ROOMS TO CREATE

DECORATING IDEAS & PROJECTS

CREATIVE
HOME
ARTS
—CLUB—

Minnetonka, Minnesota

ROOMS TO CREATE
DECORATING IDEAS & PROJECTS

Printed in 2006.

Published by North American Membership Group under license from International Masters Publishers, Inc.

Tom Carpenter
Creative Director

Heather Koshiol
Managing Editor

Gina Germ
Book Design & Production

2 3 4 5 6 / 08 07 06 05
ISBN 1-58159-236-1
© 2004 Creative Home Arts Club

Creative Home Arts Club
12301 Whitewater Drive
Minnetonka, MN 55343
www.creativehomeartsclub.com

CONTENTS

INTRODUCTION

Welcome to
ROOMS TO CREATE

Your guide to
DECORATING IDEAS & PROJECTS

When it comes to decorating your home, choosing a theme you like is important. But once you get serious about bringing your creative vision to life, you can't tackle your whole house at once. It takes an organized approach to transform your home room-by-room.

In today's home, every room serves many different purposes throughout the course of the day. The variety of rooms in your home—and the variety of family members using them—calls for creative use of space and many decorating ideas.

That's why we put together *Rooms to Create*. This photo-packed book brings you dozens of *Decorating Ideas & Projects* throughout its 160 lively and colorful pages. *Rooms to Create* gives you plenty of strategies to help you plan your home decorating schemes … then guides you to success through each step as you create the elements of your plan.

You'll see how to *Utilize Color* in all aspects of beautifying your home's interior. Then *Discover Solutions* to the decorating challenges we all run into. And see how to *Create Style* using a variety of techniques (all demonstrated in full and clear detail). Along with ideas and concepts, you'll find dozens of projects—complete with materials lists, diagrams, pattern templates, step-by-step pictures and a photograph of each finished creation.

From bedrooms, bathrooms, kitchen and dining areas to living room, den, family room and home office, you have *Rooms to Create*. And we're proud to bring you the *Decorating Ideas & Projects* you need to transform your home.

CREATIVE
HOME
ARTS
—CLUB—

UTILIZE
COLOR

Color forms the basis for any decorating project—from an accent or accessory you're creating for a room, to the walls themselves, and everything in between! Here's how to make color work for you as you decorate the rooms of your home. Chapters include:

- *Creating Seasonal Color Changes*
- *Trimming a Room with Color*
- *Unifying Mismatched Furniture with Color*

CREATING SEASONAL COLOR CHANGES

Simple color changes quickly transform a room to reflect the changing seasons.

MAKING IT WORK

Changing a room's appearance automatically lifts our spirits and heightens the mood of the season.

Simply Summer

• Cool shades of blue with shots of sunny yellow make cheerful accents against a clean, crisp, white background.

• **Simple curtains** (page 10) are best for summer. Blinds keep out the heat and damaging UV rays.

Warmed-Up Winter

• Textured fabrics and deep, dark colors create a cozy and warm retreat from the winter chill.

• Using **slipcovers** (page 12) is an easy way to transform a room's furnishings. The solid sofa color creates a focal point and sends a warm and inviting message.

VARIATIONS ON A THEME

Autumnal Elegance

Romance of Spring

• The rich, warm colors of autumn make a lasting impression and add romantic color to this inviting bedroom. A neutral **bed skirt** (page 14) and pillow shams can work throughout the year.

• Floor-length **layered curtains** (page 16) hung under a simple valance warm up the windows and ward off drafts from gusty fall winds. Sheers covering the window add softness and a touch of privacy to the room.

• Rejuvenate your home for spring by shedding winter weight and opening up rooms to warm sunlight and sweet-smelling breezes.

• Pack away heavy drapes in favor of soft sheers and a simple valance.

WRAPPED IN COZY COMFORT

This simple **tab-top canopy** (page 18) not only looks warm and snug—it insulates the room as well.
• Lined fabric, with generous gathering to trap more air, prevents cold air from seeping through the walls.
• As an added bonus, layered fabrics also deaden outside noises that would otherwise disturb a peaceful slumber.
• Even without a canopy bed, this treatment is still worth considering. Create "wall curtains" by hanging drapes from curtain rods placed at the ceiling line.
• Use big splashes of rich, warm color to give the entire room a feeling of coziness. Lots of pillows at the head of the bed and a duvet add to the warm and cozy feeling.

BORDERED CURTAINS

Transform a simple curtain to add color and style to your window treatments.

YOU WILL NEED

- ❏ COORDINATING DECORATIVE FABRICS
- ❏ LINING FABRIC
- ❏ MATCHING THREAD
- ❏ PINS & NEEDLE
- ❏ SHEARS
- ❏ SEWING MACHINE
- ❏ IRON

BEFORE YOU BEGIN

Look for fabric groupings designed for pattern mixing to ensure color, design and fabric care compatibility.

Determining Yardage

- Measure the length of the curtain rod; multiply by two to allow for fullness. The width of one panel equals half this width less two times the vertical border width; add 1 inch for seam allowances.
- The panel length equals the measurement from the rod bottom (or desired start of top panel edge) to desired length less two times the width of the border; add 1 inch for seam allowances.
- For border fabric, add the length of the curtain panel plus four times the depth of the horizontal border.
- For tabs, calculate how many you will need based on positioning them 4 to 6 inches apart. Cut fabric for each tab 6 inches wide and 12 inches long.
- For lining, determine total curtain panel dimensions. Multiply by two panels.

Sewing Instructions

All seam allowances when sewing home decorating projects are ½ inch, unless stated otherwise.

Adding a Fabric Border

For a dramatic look, use contrasting fabrics. A solid curtain with a printed border commands attention. A solid border tends to frame the curtain and add emphasis to a printed curtain.

Pattern mixing gives a designer touch to a room. Add checks, stripes or plaids to a plain or floral curtain. Cut the border on the bias (a 45° angle to the straight edge) for a new look.

The width of the border can vary from 1 to 5 inches. Consider the size of the window to plan the curtain and border proportion. Smaller windows look best with narrower borders.

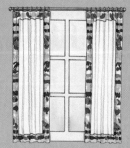

MAKING BORDERED CURTAINS

1 Cut curtain panels to size (Before you Begin). Cut lengthwise border strips equal in length to curtain panels and 2 times the width plus 1 inch. With right sides together, pin and stitch border strips to each side of both panels. Press seams open.

2 With lengthwise borders extending, cut horizontal borders the width of panel plus borders. With right sides together, pin and stitch top and bottom borders to panel and extended borders. Press open.

3 Cut tabs 6 inches wide by 12 inches long (Before you Begin). Make as many tabs as needed to fit evenly across top of each panel. Fold tab in half lengthwise, right sides together. Stitch, leaving short ends open. Turn tab right side out; press.

4 Baste ends of tabs together. Fold tabs in half. On right side of curtain panel, space tabs evenly across top edge, positioning one tab at each corner. Raw edges even, baste or pin tabs in place.

5 Cut lining panels same size as curtain panels including borders. With right sides together, pin lining to curtain along all outer edges, making sure tabs are clear of stitching area. Leave an opening along bottom edge.

6 Stitch lining to bordered curtain panel, leaving an 18- to 24-inch opening on bottom edge for turning panel right side out. Trim seam allowances and clip corners. Turn panel right side out; press. Fold raw edges of opening to the inside. Slipstitch opening closed. Check that lining lays flat; press. Put rod through tabs and hang, adjusting fullness for desired look.

SIMPLE SLIPCOVERS

Give your room a seasonal makeover with a quick and easy slipcover.

BEFORE YOU BEGIN

This slipcover is a piece of draped fabric, tucked into the couch crevices and finished with a skirt.

Determining Yardage

For slipcover, pin around perimeter of sofa where skirt will be attached. To determine width, measure from pins on back of sofa, up and over back rest and seat to front pins. To determine length, measure from side pins over arm, across seat and down other arm to pins on opposite side. Add 14 inches to each measurement for tuck-in allowance and hems.

For ruffled skirt length, measure from pins to floor; add 4 inches for hem and casing. For skirt width, measure perimeter of sofa around pins; multiply by 3. Cut enough panels to stitch together to equal skirt width.

For elastic length, measure perimeter plus 1 inch.

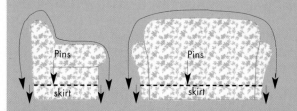

Fabric Selection

Tightly woven fabrics are best for this slipcover. King-size bedsheets made of a 50/50 polyester/cotton blend are a good choice due to their size and wrinkle resistance. Decorator fabrics, seersucker, gingham, lightweight broadcloth and polished cotton are also good choices to consider.

Upholstery Pins

Specialty pins are used to secure the slipcover to existing upholstery. A corkscrew pin with only a small transparent button visible on the right side is screwed through the fabric into upholstery.

SEWING A SIMPLE SLIPCOVER

1 For slip cover, piece fabric if necessary. Join pieces so seams are inconspicuous on finished slipcover. Do not position a seam in center of cover. To hem outer edges, turn under 1 inch; press. Turn under 1 inch again; press. Stitch near inner fold.

2 For ruffled skirt, join skirt panels along short edges. To hem lower edge, turn under 1 inch; press. Turn under 1 inch again; press. Stitch near inner fold. For elastic casing, press under ½ inch along upper edge; press under 1½ inches from first fold. Stitch near inner fold.

3 Carefully open casing to insert elastic. Attach large safety pin to end of elastic to help feed elastic through casing. Stitch elastic ends together, overlapping about ½ inch; tuck into casing. Stitch opening closed.

4 Center slipcover on sofa, right side up. Smooth fabric over back; pin in place. Pull fabric over arms; tuck into crevices. Keep fabric straight and smooth across back and top of arms. Secure with upholstery pins.

5 Smooth fabric over arms, working excess fullness toward corners. Fold or pleat excess fabric over each arm; adjust fullness evenly; pin into place. Hand baste pleats for additional security.

6 Slip skirt over sofa. Use upholstery pins to hold in place; gathers will cover pins. Adjust gathers so seams are hidden. Check that corners do not appear skimpy and gathers fall evenly across sofa.

DECORATOR BED SKIRT

Adding a skirt to your bed can create a subtly elegant look or add a splash of color.

BEFORE YOU BEGIN

The "deck" of a bed skirt is the flat fabric that goes across the bed between the box spring and mattress.

Fabric Measurements

Before constructing the skirt, prepare the deck piece, which may be cut from a flat sheet, or pieced muslin or fabric. Measure the length and width of the box spring and add 1 inch to each for seam allowance. Prewash deck fabric; then cut to size. If necessary, piece lengths of fabric for width; press seams open.

• Determine the length of the skirt by measuring from the top of the box spring to the floor. Add 4½ inches to that amount for seam allowance and hem allowance.

• Determine the width of the skirt by measuring around the sides and foot of the bed. For queen, full and twin beds, add 10 inches for seams and hems; for a king, add 12 inches.

• To plan the pleats, determine the depth of each pleat—generally 4 inches (A), and the distance between each pleat (B); the distance between pleats is usually twice the pleat depth. Plan the pleats to fall evenly on three sides of the box spring; you may have to adjust pleat widths to fit a full number of pleats across each side.

• For average fullness, multiply the measurement of the sides and foot of the bed by three. This measurement determines the width of the bed skirt fabric required. Add this amount to the 10 inches or 12 inches discussed earlier to determine the total dust ruffle width.

• Construct the bed skirt as one continuous skirt with a pleat falling at each corner. If you need to work around bedposts, make 3 separate panels with split corners.

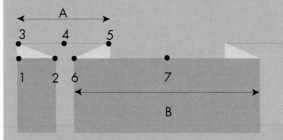

Sewing Instructions

All seam allowances when sewing home decorating projects are ½ inch, unless stated otherwise.

SEWING A BED SKIRT

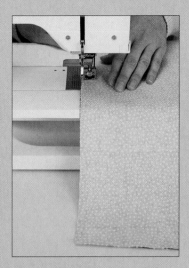

HANDY HINTS

For a quick, custom-fit ruffle, use special box pleat/folding tape rather than folding and basting pleats individually. Flatten the pleats before stitching to the deck.

DOLLAR SENSE

If you are short of fabric, add a coordinating color or print to the inside of the pleats.

1 Match patterns right sides together and sew bed skirt pieces together. If openings are needed for bedposts, create 3 panels, based on the measurements of each side and foot of mattress. Press seams open.

2 Turn up hem 2 inches along lower edge; press. Turn up 2 inches again; press. Turn up side hems 1 inch for each end and each corner, if needed; press. Turn up 1 inch again; press. Stitch hems along inner edge of folds. Cut flat sheet or fabric for deck (Before you Begin).

3 At middle of one side, center first pleat. Place seven marks for each pleat (Before you Begin). Mark 6 is the point from which to measure distance between pleats. Continue around skirt, marking all pleats. Distance between pleats may need to be adjusted near corners.

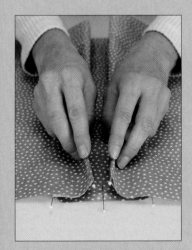

4 With right sides together, match points 2 and 6 with center point 4. Points 1 and 3 should align, as should points 5 and 7. Press entire length of pleat to hold in place and machine baste along upper edge.

5 Pin skirt to deck at sides and end. At corners, clip seam allowance up to basting line, making it easier to stitch. Stitch in place. Place bed skirt on box spring, positioning openings around bedposts.

LAYERED CURTAINS

Layer window treatments for a decorator look you can change with the seasons.

YOU WILL NEED

❏ FABRIC
❏ SEWING MACHINE
❏ PINS, THREAD & NEEDLE
❏ TOPSTITCHING THREAD
❏ WINDOW HARDWARE
❏ TAILOR'S CHALK
❏ IRON
❏ SHEARS

BEFORE YOU BEGIN

Planning is key to layering curtains successfully.

Measuring the Window Area

Install the window hardware before carefully measuring for fabric yardage of each curtain piece.

Finished curtain length equals the measurement from the top of the rod to the point where the hem edge will fall.

Finished curtain width equals the measurement of the length of curtain rod—multiply that amount by 3 for sheers and lightweights or by 2 for heavier fabrics.

Finished swag length equals the curtain rod length plus double the length of the hanging side edge. Finished swag width will equal the fabric width minus 3 inches.

Determining Yardage

For the curtains, add 9½ inches plus the diameter of the rod to the finished length. Then multiply that number by the number of fabric widths needed for desired fullness.

For the swag, use at least 45-inch-wide fabric that measures the finished swag length (width of swag from rod edge to rod edge plus twice the length of the hanging side edge) plus 4 inches.

Mark the gathering lines once you have determined how long you want the hanging side edge (longest point, below) and where you want the side edge to start higher up the window (shortest length of side edge, below).

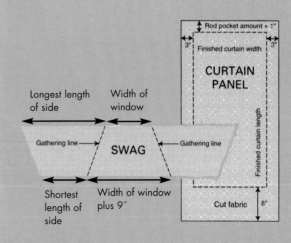

MAKING LAYERED CURTAINS

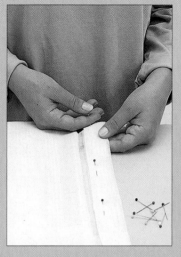

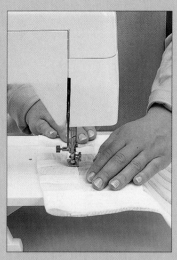

1 Cut curtain panels; piece if necessary to obtain desired fullness. To make double hem at bottom edge, fold 4 inches to wrong side; press. Fold another 4 inches and press again. Stitch along inner fold.

2 For side hems, fold 1½ inches to wrong side; press. Fold under 1½ inches again; press. Stitch along inner fold. For smooth hem edges, make first fold slightly less than 1½ inches so that the cut end doesn't bunch in the second fold.

3 Width of rod pocket opening equals diameter of rod plus 1½ inches. Fold upper edge under about ½ inch; press. Fold under width of rod pocket opening plus about 1 inch ease; press. Stitch along inner fold, leaving side edges open.

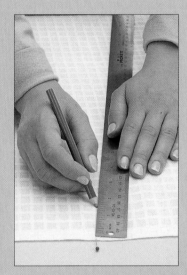

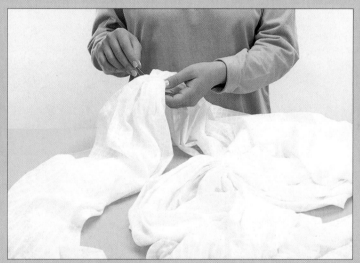

4 Make 1-inch double-fold hems along all edges of swag stitching along inner fold; press. Use tailor's chalk to mark placement of gathering stitches clearly (Before you Begin).

5 Secure end of topstitching thread at one edge of markings. Using a hand needle, run a gathering stitch through one diagonal marking line. Pull thread to gather; knot securely. Repeat process on other diagonal line. Hang curtains on metal curtain rod. Hang swag over decorative curtain rod. Adjust swag so top edge is taut and lower edge drapes gracefully; adjust sides into soft folds.

TAB-TOP BED CANOPY

Fabric panels create a relaxing retreat and can easily be updated for changing seasons.

BEFORE YOU BEGIN

You will need to hang the canopy hardware in order to determine the amount of fabric to buy.

Securing Hardware

There are numerous hardware styles suitable for hanging a canopy. This C-shaped wrought iron ring is mounted to the wall with toggle bolts. Bolts or screws are usually provided by the manufacturer.

If your fabric is particularly heavy, further secure the ring with a ceiling hook and some type of decorative chain.

Determining Canopy Length

Mount chosen hardware on wall directly over head of bed, about 7 feet from floor.

Hang a string from ring over side of bed to floor or to desired finished length. Adjust string to emulate desired drape of canopy. Mark point on string where actual canopy panel will begin (accounting for length of tied tabs). Measure string from marking to lower edge to determine length of finished canopy.

Yardage and Cutting Directions

Panel cutting length: Add 1 inch to canopy length for seam allowances.

Number of fabric widths: Generally one fabric width is satisfactory for each panel no matter what size bed. If fabric is sheer or especially soft, consider making the panels wider for more fullness.

Yardage required for face fabric and lining: Panel cutting length times number of fabric widths equals fabric length in inches.

For tabs, add 18 inches for tabs of fabric only (not lining). To determine number of tabs needed, plan to place each set of tabs 4 to 6 inches apart. (Don't forget to figure 2 tabs per set so you can tie them together onto the ring.)

Divide by 36 inches to determine yards needed. Allow extra yardage for pattern matching.

Sewing Instructions

All seam allowances when sewing home decorating

projects are ½ inch, unless stated otherwise.

SEWING A TAB-TOP CANOPY

1 Cut fabric for tabs 6 inches wide by 18 inches long. With right sides together, fold tab pieces in half lengthwise. Sew one short end, pivot at corner and continue stitching down long cut edge. Do not stitch other short end.

2 Trim corners diagonally. Turn tabs right side out. Use straight pin or bodkin to turn corners completely; press. Make enough tabs so there are two tabs for each place tabs are sewn to canopy edge.

3 Pin tabs to right side of canopy with raw edges even and tabs extending into body of fabric. Position outside tabs ⅝ inch from side edges and remaining tabs evenly across width; machine baste in place.

HANDY HINTS

Lining the canopy is important because the wrong side is visible to anyone lying in the bed. Consider a contrasting fabric for a lining that provides design interest.

DOLLAR SENSE

Coordinating bedsheets are perfect fabrics for bed canopies. They are often wide enough to eliminate the need for piecing and they are relatively inexpensive.

4 With right sides together and tabs in between, pin lining to fabric with all edges even. Making sure loose ends of tabs do not get caught in stitching, stitch around all sides, leaving a 6-inch opening on bottom edge.

5 Trim corners on diagonal. Turn panel right side out. Hand stitch opening closed; press. To hang canopy, tie tabs into square knots over hardware. Tie tabs at equal lengths so top is uniform and bottom edge of canopy hangs straight.

TRIMMING A ROOM WITH COLOR

Calling out wooden trim and moldings with paint can add a whole new dimension to a room.

Making it Work

Highlight the door frames in one color and use muted shades for walls and doors to add visual interest to a space.

Neutral Contrast

• Every color appears to be more striking when set against a lighter one. Even though the gray of the **moldings** (page 24) isn't bold, placed against the pale tint of pink, it creates a strong contrast.

• Outlining shapes with color helps break up the area and avoid the long "runway" look that plagues so many hallways.

• The pale colors of the walls and doors make limited space appear to open up. Ample lighting overhead makes the hallway even more friendly.

• Pale pink walls in one area prevent the hallway from becoming a bland all-white expanse.

• Pure white paint can often be too stark and bright. For these doors, a hint of the surrounding molding color was added to white. The result is a softer, mellower look than bright white doors would have been.

Variation on a Theme

Cool Blue Charm

• There is no need to use the same color on each piece of trim in the room. For a harmonious look that still holds interest, choose different shades of one color from the same paint chip.

• For cool white **wood paneling** (page 26) that blends smoothly with the soft blue trim, add some blue to white paint. **Molding panels** (page 34) offer a classic alternative to tongue-and-groove paneling.

• To avoid an awkward break in the line of color, paint the **picture or chair rail** (page 28) and **window frame** (page 22) the same color but choose a slightly darker shade for the trim around the window panes. A **whimsical word border** (page 30) is another colorful way to utilize a chair rail.

• Pick up the colors of the trim in accessories such as the window valance, rug, seat cushion and pottery display.

FINISHING TOUCHES

Make **molding trims** (pages 24 and 32) all the more appealing by replacing plain treatments with decorative pieces.
• Moldings come in a multitude of styles and materials. Kits with pre-mitered pieces can be purchased at lumberyards and home centers.
• Instead of a plain door casing, opt for elegant ridges (below). The corner piece, comes in a variety of designs as well.

COLORBLOCKED WINDOW FRAMES

Simple paint patterns transform your windows into works of art.

BEFORE YOU BEGIN

Use semigloss oil-based enamel paints for painting interior trim such as windows. When dry, these paints are durable and easy to clean.

Working with Windows

• Remove metal hardware from the windows before painting. Clean the hardware before reattaching it to the window.
• Some windows have pop-out mullion bars. Simply remove the bars to paint; reinsert when dry.
• If a window does not open smoothly, remove it from the frame, clean the side tracks, then reposition it in the frame.
• To remove tape residue and other grime from the glass, mix two parts ammonia with one part water, rub onto the glass, then wipe off with a lint-free cloth.

Color Coordination

Make a window diagram (above). Consider your room's decor, and experiment with different paint colors and both symmetrical and asymmetrical designs. Follow your window diagram when painting the mullion bars and frame.

When colorblocking, choose colors that suggest a specific time period, such as purple and deep burgundy for the Victorian era.

Use your window to mimic famous works of art. For example, painting with primary colors offers the look of Mondrian; soft colors are reminiscent of Monet.

Use colors that match the fabric in your curtains or other colors in your decor. For accuracy, have the paint mixed to match the actual wallpaper or fabric sample.

Paint the mullion bars and the outside of the frame with the softest or palest color in the palette. A darker color will visually divide the window into small sections. Save the boldest color in your palette to paint the window trim; it will make the window appear larger.

Painting Hints

Paint adheres best to a clean, dry smooth surface.
• Sand the window frame with medium-grade sandpaper to remove chipped and old paint. Remove any grit by wiping off with a soft, damp cloth or tack cloth.
• Use a paint scraper to remove stubborn patches of paint from the window frame.
• If there are many coats of paint, use a liquid chemical stripping product.
• If desired, prime the frame before painting.

COLORBLOCKING A WINDOW FRAME

HANDY HINTS

To remove paint drips and brush marks from glass panes, lift the protective tape after the paint has dried.

1 Apply painter's masking tape around mullion bars for protection. Following your diagram (Before you Begin), paint mullion bars in the first color with small paintbrush. Begin at top left corner of window and work left to right.

2 Continue to paint all mullion bars according to diagram, except those in center; let dry. Reposition tape to outline inside of window frame and center bars. Paint frame and center bars with second color and let dry.

3 Reposition masking tape to form outline around edges of outside window frame. Apply additional strip of tape around outside of window to keep last color of paint from accidentally brushing onto wall.

With the sharp, straight edge of a razor blade, scrape the pane at an angle. Continue until all the paint has chipped off.

4 Using small paintbrush and following diagram, paint entire window frame with last color of paint. Let dry completely. If necessary, apply second coat of paint for even coverage. When all coats of paint are dry, remove all masking tape from window.

DECORATIVE CEILING MOLDING

Trimming a room with decorative molding creates a crowning effect.

BEFORE YOU BEGIN

Hanging molding is a project that adds new interest around the top of a room. Follow these installation hints to help get the job done.

Trim Tips

• Always add 10% to your estimates when buying trim to allow for waste.
• To keep molding from slipping, line your miter box with sandpaper.
• If gluing joints together, let excess glue dry, then chisel or chip it away. Smudged glue can cause imperfections in the paint job.
• Paint molding before installing, then touch up afterwards.
• Sink nails with a nail set instead of a hammer. This will prevent dimpling the molding with the hammer.

Designing with Molding

• Crown molding is available in many different styles (right). There are no steadfast rules for choosing a style—just choose a molding that fits your room proportions and decorating scheme.
• The higher the ceiling, the wider the crown molding can be. Eight-foot-high ceilings generally have 4- to 6-inch molding, while 9-foot ceilings have crowns of up to 9 inches.
• Crown molding can be combined with other molding accents to create different effects. Try mixing crown molding, picture molding and ceiling rosettes for an elegant look (right).

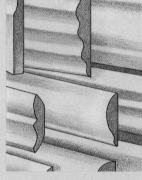

YOU WILL NEED

❏ ½x4 PINE
❏ 2⅝-INCH CROWN MOLDING
❏ ¾-INCH SHOE MOLDING
❏ 1-INCH STEP MOLDING
❏ CHALK LINE
❏ MITER BOX & SAW
❏ HAMMER, NAILS & NAIL SET
❏ PAINT & PAINTBRUSH
❏ CLEAN CLOTH
❏ SANDPAPER
❏ WOOD PUTTY

INSTALLING CEILING MOLDING

1 Measure and mark length of molding. Place upside down in a miter box and cut each end at a 45° angle. Repeat with remaining molding, making sure cuts for each joint are opposite each other and equal 90°.

2 Lightly sand each strip of molding and wipe clean with a damp cloth. Paint each strip, brushing horizontally. Let dry completely, then apply another coat. Make sure top and bottom edges are painted.

3 Nail ½x4 pine to ceiling, ½ inch away from wall. Using chalk line, draw a line on wall 1½ inches down from ceiling. Fasten line at one end. Hold other end taut. Pull string back and then release so chalked string hits wall.

4 Nail second piece of ½x4 pine to wall, aligning top of wood with chalk line. For security, use nails along top and bottom of wood. Continue around wall, making sure all corners are neatly joined.

5 Attach crown molding around top of wall. Align molding top with top of wall, flush against ½x4 pine on ceiling; bottom will overlap ½x4 pine on wall. Ensure corners of molding strips join in neat 90° angles.

6 Attach strips of shoe molding directly under crown molding, on top of ½x4 pine. Then attach strips of step molding to wall, flush with bottom of ½x4 pine. Make sure all joints are neat 90° angles. Continue putting up molding until entire circumference of room is complete. Touch up molding where necessary, and cover all nail heads with wood putty and a dab of paint to match the molding piece.

ATTRACTIVE WOOD PANELING

Attractive and practical, paneling adds color and dimension to any room.

You Will Need

❑ Furring strips
❑ Tongue & groove panels
❑ Baseboard & chair rail moldings
❑ Hammer, nails & nail set
❑ Drill & screws
❑ Saw & level
❑ Sandpaper & wood filler
❑ Pencil, tape measure & ruler
❑ Primer, paint & varnish

BEFORE YOU BEGIN

Paneling hides wall flaws and provides a tough finish for heavy-traffic areas.

Application

Different wall types require different application methods:
• For wallboard, tap to find out where wall studs are (usually 16 inches apart). If possible, drill into studs.

Otherwise, drill toggle bolts into wallboard.
• For brick and plaster, you will need a masonry drill bit, masonry screws and wall plugs.

Preparation

Measure wall sections (from door to corner or corner to window) and cut furring strips to fit, mitering the corners. Nail into wall studs or, to attach strips to brick or plaster, drill starter holes into the strips at 18-inch intervals.

Countersink holes (below) so screws won't protrude.

Trim Option

Decorate a dining area with shelf-trimmed paneled walls.
• Nail three furring strips to the wall between baseboard and top of panels to support extra panel height.

• Screw back of painted shelf to top furring strip and support shelf front with matching decorative brackets.

INSTALLING TONGUE-AND-GROOVE PANELING

1 Decide on the height of the paneling. (Common panel height for chair molding is 30 to 40 inches.) Measure from the floor to this point and mark at regular intervals along the wall. Join the marks together with a faint pencil line, using a level to keep it straight.

2 Measure a second, lower line for center furring strip. Hold furring strips to wall, tops on pencil line. Mark and drill starter holes, if necessary. Nail or screw furring strip to wall at these marks.

3 Cut new, shallow baseboard to fit over old one. Predrill small holes along the top and bottom at 18-inch intervals. Nail to the old baseboard through predrilled holes, ensuring that the nail heads are countersunk.

4 Size panels by resting one end on the new baseboard and marking the level of the top of the furring strip at the other end. Cut to fit. Measure and cut each panel in its place in case floor slopes slightly.

5 Starting in corner, place first panel, tongue-side to wall. Nail in place at top and center furring strips and at old baseboard. Now butt adjoining corner panel, groove-side to first, and fasten. Continue.

6 Finish paneling around the room. Then cut chair rail to fit, mitering corners. Rail can be plain or decorative but should be deep enough to cover depth of panel and furring strip with a small overlap. Nail in place.

7 Use a nail set to hammer in any protruding nail heads. Fill holes and seal joint along chair rail and top of panels with wood filler. When dry, sand any rough edges, prime and paint. Protect with two coats of varnish.

HANDY HINTS

For long furring strips, get a friend to hold one end when nailing the strips to the wall. Or hammer a nail into the wall to rest one end on while you work. The nail hole will be covered by paneling.

TAKE NOTE

Tongue-and-groove panels are easy to slot together—until the last one. If it needs to be cut to fit, use a handsaw or have a lumber-yard cut it for you. When attaching it, leave the neighboring panel unattached so you can pull it forward to slide end panel in; then position both panels back in place and nail.

QUICK FIX

Wainscot paneling, available at many home improvement stores, is shaped with beaded profiles to look like tongue-and-groove boards. It is inexpensive, available in many styles and quality levels, and easy to install.

SIMPLE ADDED CHAIR RAILS

Add painted molding to divide wall space decoratively.

BEFORE YOU BEGIN

To give moldings a professional appearance, miter cut edges where they meet at internal and external corners.

Preparing Wall Surfaces

Prepare walls as for any other wall treatment. Apply paint or hang wallpaper after hanging the molding.

Or attach the molding, set and fill nail holes, and then paint entire wall.

Measuring and Positioning

Measure the width of each wall. Add a few inches to each length for mitering.
• Molding is available in lengths up to 16 feet. Use one length per wall to minimize having to join pieces.

• Chair rails (without paneling) are typically positioned 32 to 36 inches from the floor.
• Rails can be positioned higher, but avoid cutting the wall in half.

Mitering Corners

Miter cuts for squared corners are made at a 40° angle.

Measure the molding rail and lightly mark the end where it should be cut.

Clamp rail on its edge with right side facing out to one side of miter box.

Line up the pencil mark with the cut line on the miter box. Cut through the rail; sand to smooth edges.

Cut adjoining rail with an opposite miter cut (below).

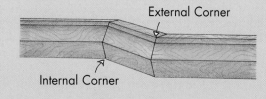

External Corner

Internal Corner

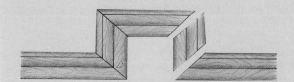

Piecing Mitered Corners

POSITIONING MOLDING FOR RAILS

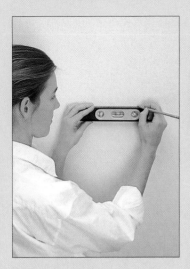

1 Measure up from the floor or the baseboards to determine chair rail placement. Mark points where rail will be attached. Join marks using a level to form a horizontal guideline. Adjust at corners.

2 Measure wall length. Cut first rail 2 inches longer than required. Start with a square butt edge against a door or window casing. Mark the wall length onto the rail. Miter cut the end of the rail at mark.

3 Locate wall studs (normally 16 inches apart). Hold the rail in exact position (with help) and drill starter holes through molding into wall at wall studs. Holes should be slightly smaller than diameter of nails.

4 Nail the rail in place with finishing nails. To avoid denting the rail, do not drive nails all the way in. This will also make it easier to remove the nail if the rail has been positioned incorrectly.

5 Measure and mark length on the second rail. Cut rail edge using miter box so edge dovetails snugly up against the end of the first rail. If necessary, lightly sand the rail edges before fitting together.

6 Continue hanging one rail at a time. When all rails are in position, set nails below wood surface using a hammer and nail set. Fill in holes and gaps with spackling compound. Sand, wipe off dust and paint. If staining instead, fill holes with wood putty.

Whimsical Word Border

A colorful, decorative message adds a touch of whimsy to a wall.

Letters are easier to paint than complicated designs or motifs, and they fill a blank space in a unique and cheerful way.

Using the Template

Nursery rhymes never go out of style. These stylized letters are simplistic and childlike, perfect for a nursery or playroom. To reproduce the design featured here, measure the area to be filled with lettering, and enlarge the letters on a photocopier until the letters are large enough to fill the space.

HUMPTY DUMPTY SAT ON A WALL

Finding the Words

• Create your own lettering or copy lettering from any source onto the wall. For inspiration, look at typeface books, magazine headlines or alphabet stencils in different styles.
• Choose the words you want. If they are already printed in the desired type style, use a photocopier to enlarge each letter.

• If you cannot find words in a style you like, ask a print shop to write out the saying in different styles, and then enlarge to the desired size to create a pattern.

YOU WILL NEED

❑ TAPE MEASURE
❑ METAL STRAIGHTEDGE
❑ PENCIL & PAPER
❑ LATEX PAINT
❑ FOAM BRUSHES
❑ MASKING TAPE
❑ DECORATIVE MOLDING
❑ WOOD GLUE
❑ LEVEL
❑ HAMMER, FINISHING
   NAILS & NAIL SET

WRITING ON THE WALL

1 Prepare wall. Measure height of letters or pattern; use straightedge and pencil to measure and mark top and bottom boundaries. Mark again 1 inch outside both markings for molding strip placements.

2 To transfer lettering to wall, scribble over reverse side of each letter with a soft lead pencil. Use masking tape to hold pattern in position on wall, right side up. Trace over outline of each letter with pencil.

3 Remove pattern from wall. Use a foam brush and latex paint to fill in pencil outlines of letters. Paint each letter in a different color; take care not to smudge wet letters when painting adjacent ones.

TAKE NOTE

Use matte paints for lettering. Gloss paints have a sheen which can be distracting and may make the letters hard to read from certain angles.

OOPS

Mistakes made with water-based paint can be rectified as long as the paint has not dried. Wipe off the mistake with a damp cloth and repaint once the area has completely dried.

4 Let paint dry. Cut molding strips to desired length. If molding is unfinished, paint it a color to match wall. Use wood glue to adhere molding in place along markings. Use a level to check that molding is straight; secure with finishing nails. Use nail set to countersink nails. Fill holes with putty; sand smooth when dry.

5 Mask outside edges of molding, leaving area to be painted exposed. Paint bands of alternating color along whole length of both molding strips. Width of each band should be width of foam brush. Let paint dry, then remove masking tape. Reapply masking tape to protect molding, then paint rest of wall in a color that matches colors used on painted words. Apply several coats of polyurethane over lettering and molding.

FORMAL FINISHED MOLDINGS

Use paint to mimic the rich look of burled wood on a chair rail.

YOU WILL NEED

- ❏ WOOD MOLDING
- ❏ PRIMER & PAINT THINNER
- ❏ TAN SEMI-GLOSS PAINT
- ❏ PECAN POLY/STAIN MIX
- ❏ BURNT UMBER POLY/STAIN MIX
- ❏ FOAM BRUSHES & ARTIST'S BRUSHES
- ❏ PLASTIC WRAP
- ❏ RUBBER GLOVES
- ❏ POLYURETHANE
- ❏ WOOD PUTTY (OPTIONAL)

BEFORE YOU BEGIN

Prior to faux painting, lightly sand and prime. Apply two coats of tan semigloss paint as a base, drying thoroughly after each coat.

Moldings Selection

Molding styles range from flat baseboards to ornate crown styles. Lengths of molding can extend up to 16 feet.
- Faux marbling, with its intricate veining, works best on flat, smooth surfaces. Good molding choices include flat base molding or simple styles of casing molding.
- The burled-wood paint technique is effective on chair rails and other molding with a few curves, but not too many so the painting is difficult.

- Spray-painted "stone" treatments look great on cove molding as well as highly curved crown or bed moldings.

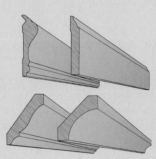

Installing the Finished Molding

- Use a pencil, level and ruler to mark placement of the molding around the room.
- Measure each wall and plan how to piece the molding with the fewest possible seams.
- Cut the molding to length, allowing a few extra inches for professional-looking mitered corners.
- Using a miter box and saw, miter the ends of the molding pieces to fit the corners.
- Nail the molding into the

studs at the penciled guides. Countersink nails. Fill holes and gaps with matching wood putty, or touch up with paint.

SIMULATING BURLED WOOD ON MOLDING

1 Holding a 1-inch-wide foam brush perpendicular to the surface, apply pecan poly/stain to the molding in short, thick stripes. Space the markings randomly and at angles, not parallel. Leave open areas.

2 Following the same procedure as in Step 1, dab darker poly/stain between first set of stripes at random angles. Allow the base color to show through between and around both colors of stripes.

3 While paint is still wet, crumple a piece of plastic wrap and blot it onto the surface, softly blending the two colors of stripes and transforming all of the sharp-edge lines into softer, more diffused patches.

4 Gently press a gloved finger into the dark patches to simulate the round and oval knots of genuine burl wood. Make one to four knots in each cluster, keeping a light and dark contrast in each knot.

5 Swirl an artist's lettering brush through the surface to create rings around knots in an irregular pattern. Aim for contrasts in knots and clusters to yield a varied surface with both "busy" and "calm" areas.

6 Load a fine artist's brush with the darker poly/stain; lightly touch the surface of each knot, slightly off center, one to four times. Touch up the surface as necessary. Let dry; finish with a coat of polyurethane.

HANDY HINTS

When making the knots in the wood with a gloved fingerprint, press gently to achieve the preferable irregular markings in the knot. Using too much pressure will allow an undesirable opaque circle of base coat to show through.

For more mitering and installation instructions, see pages 28 and 29.

TAKE NOTE

If any area looks too "busy" (overly detailed), gently feed in paint thinner from the side of the brush, allowing colors to loosen and run into each other.

ELEGANT MOLDING PANELS FOR WALLS

Ordinary walls turn dramatic when accented with painted molding panels.

BEFORE YOU BEGIN

Plan the molding panel design on paper to work out measurements.

Planning the Molding Panel

Let the room's shape dictate the shape of the panels. Consider long and lean lines, short and wide panels or combine both for a unique look that will add character to the wall.

Determine heights and widths of panels based on width of wall. Calculate equal distances between panels. Make distances from outer edge of panel to chair rail and chair rail to baseboard equal.

After compiling all the measurements, determine how much molding to purchase. Molding strips come in lengths up to 16 feet.

CREATING MOLDING PANELS

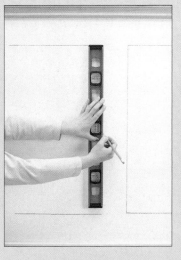

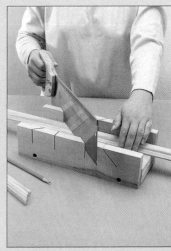

HANDY HINTS

For long molding strips, get a friend to hold one end when nailing the molding to the wall. Or, using wood glue, position the molding on the wall and then nail into place.

QUICK FIX

Molding panel kits are available at many lumber-yards and home decorating stores. They contain precut and premitered molding panels that are ready to be attached to your walls. Bring your panel measurements to the store to make sure the kit pieces will fit. They are ready to be nailed, primed and painted.

1 Prepare wall and baseboard. Measure from baseboard up to height of chair rail placement. Mark points where rail will be attached. Join marks using a level to form a horizontal guideline; nail chair rail in place.

2 Mark placement of molding panels using preplanned measurements as a guide; mark where outside edge of molding will be placed. Use a level to ensure lines are straight and at right angles to each other.

3 Cut molding pieces at 45° angles, making sure outer edges equal panel measurements. Arrange panel pieces together to ensure fit before securing to wall. Sand mitered edges to make sure they are smooth.

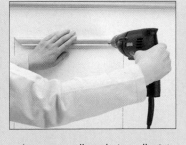

6 Using a nail set, drive nails in all the way. Use wood putty to conceal holes left in molding. Putty any corners that have open spaces. Smooth out putty surface with fine sandpaper, if necessary.

4 Locate wall studs (usually 16 inches apart). Hold molding piece in exact position (or hold in place with wood glue) and drill holes into molding strip at wall studs. Make holes slightly smaller than diameter of nails.

5 Nail molding strip into wall with finishing nails. To avoid denting the molding, do not drive nails all the way in. Continue nailing all panel pieces to wall, making sure all corners are snug and straight.

7 If you plan to paint the wall and panels one color, prep walls and prime panels before painting. If you are painting only the panels, place masking tape along edges of panels to prevent spills and smudges. Work with a small brush.

UNIFYING MISMATCHED FURNITURE WITH COLOR

Bring harmony to a mix of furniture styles and designs through the use of common colors.

MAKING IT WORK

Bring together wicker, wood and upholstered furniture under a cool color scheme of mid-range blues and greens.

Matched Set

• This odd collection of casual country furniture takes on the look of a matched set through the use of colors of the same value. The room's all-white walls provide a neutral background without distracting.

• The apple green of the **painted wicker** loveseat (page 38) echoes in the loveseat's flower-covered **cushion** (page 40) and **flanged-edge pillows** (page 42) on the slipcovered chair.

• Paint a graceful rocker in a pastel blue. Highlight it with blue and white

striped cushions and a woven throw in a blue on white windowpane motif.

• Turn an ordinary wooden bench into a decorative table by sponging on a soft blue antique glaze over creamy white.

• As a final unifying touch, add a sisal rug in broad stripes of green, one the apple green of the loveseat, the other a paler version.

VARIATION ON A THEME

Pattern Repeat

• In a small bedroom, use the same fabric to cover major furniture pieces such as the bed and the **shelving unit** (pages 44, 48).

You can also use coordinating linens to **line the back** of a shelving unit (page 46) or make a **fitted table cover** (page 50).

• Cover accent pillows in a coordinated fabric. The apparent randomness of the design in the one contrasts nicely with the regularity of the stripes in the other. Bedsheets are a solid pastel match.

VICE VERSA

• Continue the leafy **fabric pattern** (page 52), only in reverse, by transferring it to stencil paper and applying its several motifs in white to the green-painted walls.

PAINTED WICKER FURNITURE

Enhance the texture of wicker with delicate touches of color.

BEFORE YOU BEGIN

Choose colors that contrast with natural wicker. Then plan the pattern and determine the effect you want.

Planning and Preparation

When planning, keep these points in mind:
• Choose a color that is a little darker or bolder than you really want. Once the paint is diluted, it will not look as strong.
• If you are uncertain how the chosen color will look, test it on the bottom of the chair or some other surface that won't be seen.
• In a bucket, mix the latex paint with water using a ratio of 2:1. Stir the paint completely so the color and consistency are uniform. Using latex paint is important; oil paints are too messy to clean up.
• Protect the floor and work surface with lots of newspaper or some other protective covering such as a plastic tarp.
• Wicker lets a lot of paint drip through. So if painting a wicker table top, cover the shelf below.

Two Different Effects

For a subtle effect (*right*), wipe a damp cloth across the surface immediately after painting a section of the wicker. This removes most of the color from the raised areas for a gentle, faded look. Change cloths frequently for best results.

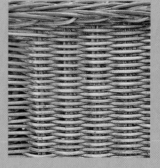

For a more painted finish (*right*), apply one or two coats, letting the paint dry completely. Then gently rub across the surface with fine grade sandpaper to expose some of the raised wicker. This treatment gives a slightly worn appearance.

PAINTING THE FURNITURE

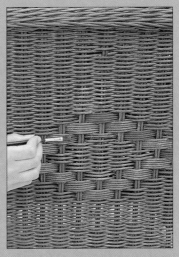

1 Put an ample amount of paint onto the brush and apply all over the wicker, making sure to get into all the cracks and crevices. Work in small sections; the paint should be wet if it is to be wiped off.

2 To create a more subtle effect, use sandpaper to wipe across the wicker immediately after painting. The color will come off the raised areas. Do one section at a time so the paint doesn't dry.

3 Choose a section of the furniture where the weave is different, and highlight with paint. Select a color that contrasts with the base color and apply using a smaller paintbrush.

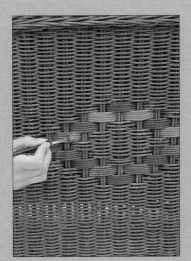

4 To complete the woven effect, select another contrasting color and paint alternating design segments. Check the color once it dries; lighter colors may need two or even three coats of paint.

5 Make sure all paint dries completely. Then, using a bristle brush, apply two or three coats of polyurethane to protect the furniture. Allow to dry thoroughly between coats; sand lightly, if necessary.

TUFTED CUSHION FOR A WICKER CHAIR

Cushions add color and comfort to a favorite wicker chair.

BEFORE YOU BEGIN

Add self-covered buttons to create a fashionable tufted cushion for your favorite wicker chair.

Making a Paper Pattern

Position a large piece of paper over the seat of the wicker chair. Using a pencil, mark the outline of the seat edges. This will determine the shape of the finished cushion. Note which is the back edge of the pattern piece.

Smooth out the paper pattern on a flat surface. To the outer edges of the pattern line, mark the distance of one half the depth measurement of the cushion plus ½ inch.

The depth measurement reflects how thick you want the cushion to be when finished. Three inches deep is a normal seat cushion depth, but consider adding another inch because some of the depth will be lost to the tufting process.

Cut along the outer marked line to create the finished pattern piece for the cushion fabric.

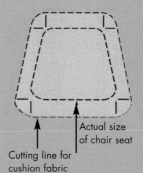

Cutting line for cushion fabric

Actual size of chair seat

Determining Fabric Yardage

Measure the width of the pattern piece. If it is less than half the width of the fabric, you will need to buy only the length of one pillow piece.

If the width of the pattern exceeds one half the width of the fabric, you will need to purchase fabric yardage equal to twice the length of the pillow.

Sewing Instructions

All seam allowances when sewing home decorating projects are ½ inch, unless stated otherwise.

Sewing the Cushion

TAKE NOTE

Choose a washable fabric and filler for a tufted pillow because the cover cannot be removed after the buttons are attached.

1 Place cushion pattern over two layers of fabric with right sides together; pin in place. Cut through all layers. Remove pattern and pin around cushion edges. Sew around all sides, leaving a 6-inch opening at center back. Follow curves and pivot at corners.

2 At front corners of pillow, with seam centered, flatten fabric and mark a line perpendicular to the seam that measures 3 inches across; do this at both corners. Stitch across marked lines. Turn cushion right side out.

3 Press cover well; it is difficult to remove wrinkles after cover is filled and buttons are sewn on. Follow manufacturer's instructions for covering buttons.

4 Fill pillow with foam chips. Use polyester batting if fabric is not heavyweight. Chips may cause lumps in lightweight fabric. Do not overstuff pillow or you will not be able to sew buttons on. Pin opening closed.

5 Decide on positioning of buttons closer together at narrower end. Stitch button thread through both sides of pillow; pull tight.

6 When all buttons are sewn in place, check to see if any more stuffing is needed to fill out the pillow. When stuffing is completed, slipstitch the pillow opening closed.

FLANGED-EDGE PILLOWS

These simple pillows are an easy way to add color and style to any setting.

BEFORE YOU BEGIN

These quick-sew pillows have wide borders created as the seams are sewn.

Measuring and Buying Fabric

Measure the pillow form and decide how wide the border will be. These blue covers were made to fit a 16-inch square pillow, with a 2-inch border. For the seam allowance, add 2 inches more to each side. The front panel of this fabric is 24¼ inches square.

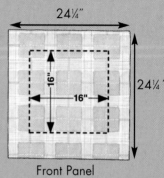

Front Panel

The back of the pillow is made from two panels of fabric. The width of each is the same as the width of the front panel. The depth of each panel should be 4¼ inches less than the depth of the front panel, 20 inches (right, A). The two panels are overlapped to form a 24¼-inch square (below, B) and stitched down each side to make up the back panel. Check that the fabric's pattern matches for a perfect finish.

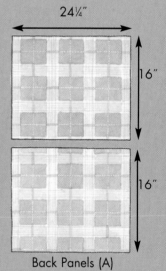

Back Panels (A)

For this 16-inch pillow with a 2-inch border, get 1⅜ yards of 45- to 54-inch-wide fabric.

For a 20-inch square pillow with a 2-inch border you will need 1⅝ yards of 45- to 54-inch-wide fabric. Be sure to add 4 inches to all measurements shown in diagrams.

Back Panels (B)

Allow extra for matching bold patterns.

Sewing the Pillow Cover

1 Cut out the front and back panels, following the cutting layout used to calculate the fabric (Before you Begin). Turn and press a ½-inch double hem across one long edge on each back panel. Pin and stitch.

2 Hemmed edges facing and wrong sides up, slide one back panel over the other until their combined depth equals that of the front panel. Baste them together down each side so they form a single panel.

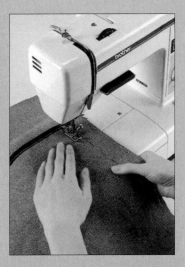

3 Position the back panels against front panel with right sides together, matching the raw edges. Pin together, then baste the seam, positioning the stitching 2 inches in from the raw edges. Machine stitch seam.

HANDY HINTS

When working with thick fabrics, make the lower back panel from a piece of the main fabric and a remnant of thinner, canvas material for the lining panel. This will reduce the amount of bulk in the cover.

OOPS

If the cover gapes open at the back when you put a pillow inside it, add tabs of hook-and-loop fastener at the center of the opening to hold the cover together.

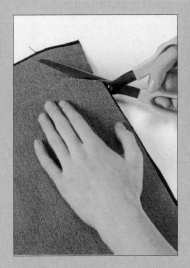

4 At each corner, trim seam allowance close to the stitching. On cotton fabrics, cut diagonally across the corner. With bulkier fabrics, trim top layer of seam allowance all around to ¼ inch.

5 Press the seams open. Turn the pillow cover right side out. Use a pair of fabric shears to poke the fabric out to form a sharp point at each corner. Press along the seams.

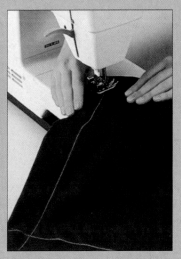

6 Finally, topstitch around the cover, positioning stitching 2 inches in from the outer edge. At each corner, lift the foot of the machine and pivot the fabric on the needle for a neat turn.

CLEVER COVER-UPS FOR SHELVING UNITS

Create instant storage that's neatly tucked inside a color-coordinated case.

YOU WILL NEED

- ❏ TAPE MEASURE
- ❏ FABRIC, THREAD & FABRIC SHEARS
- ❏ SEWING MACHINE
- ❏ BULLION TRIM
- ❏ NEEDLE & PINS
- ❏ IRON
- ❏ SMALL CURTAIN WEIGHTS (OPTIONAL)

BEFORE YOU BEGIN

To determine how much fabric to buy, accurately measure the shelving unit.

Measure Up

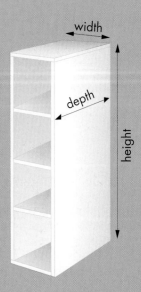

- For panel lengths, measure the height of the unit; add 8½ inches for seam and hem. For the width of the side panels, measure the depth of the unit; add 1 inch. For the back panel, measure the width of the unit; add 1 inch. For front panels, add 2 inches to the width measurement; divide in half to make two panels. For the top piece, measure the width and depth of the unit; add 1 inch to each measurement.
- For front panel facing, cut two strips 3 inches wide by panel length.
- For ties, cut four strips of fabric 36 inches long and 5 inches wide.

Alternate Opening

This cover-up's opening mimics old-fashioned roller blinds.

- For front framing edges, cut two 12-inch-wide fabric strips the height of the unit. Fold in half, right sides out; press. Stitch one to each side panel with raw edges even.
- For a top flap, fold a 20-inch-long fabric piece in half, right sides together. Stitch short sides; turn right side out. Place between top of cover-up and main front panel.
- For the main front panel, cut two pieces of fabric the width of the front plus 1 inch. Right sides together, stitch at sides and lower edge; turn and press. Pin raw edge of opening to top of cover-up between front framing edges and top.
- For ties, cut four fabric strips 5 inches wide and the length of the unit. Stitch each tie right sides together; turn and press. Place main front panel between each set of ties.

MAKING A SHELVING UNIT COVER-UP

HANDY HINTS

Add small curtain weights to the hem of the front panels to help them hang straight and stay in place.

1 Fold tie strips in half lengthwise with right sides together and raw edges even; pin. Cut one end at an angle. Starting at point, stitch point and long edge. Trim corners, turn; press. Repeat for all remaining ties.

2 Divide and mark length of front panels by three. Pin ties at mark on right side of fabric of each panel; machine baste. Pin facing on top with right sides together and raw edges even; stitch, keeping points free.

3 With right sides together and raw edges even, pin front panels to side panels and side panels to back panels; stitch. Lay panels on flat surface and press all seams open, including front facing seam.

TAKE NOTE

All seam allowances when sewing home decorating projects are ½ inch, unless stated otherwise.

DOLLAR SENSE

Get the most fabric for your money by purchasing decorative sheets instead of fabric to make the cover-up. A narrow cover-up can be made easily from one king size sheet.

4 Fold under a 4-inch double hem at bottom edge of panels and front facing, pin in place. Press flat. With matching thread, stitch panel hem in place using machine hem stitch, or slipstitch by hand.

5 Fold each facing to wrong side of each front panel and press flat. Pin in place, then slipstitch facing to panel to secure, making sure that stitches are invisible from front of fabric.

6 With right sides together and raw edges even, pin top of front panels to width edge of top piece; continue to pin sides and back to top; machine stitch in place. Trim corners, press seams open.

7 Working on flat surface and starting at a back corner of fabric, pin bullion trim around seam at top of cover-up to ensure that trim hangs smoothly. Turn under raw edges of ends of trim for clean finish. Using matching thread, handstich bullion trim in place.

FABRIC-LINED SHELVING

A colorful fabric backdrop is an attractive way to coordinate furniture with your décor.

BEFORE YOU BEGIN

Pattern size plays a major role in the choice of fabrics. When placing fabric on the shelf, be sure to display the pattern to its best advantage.

Pattern Repeats

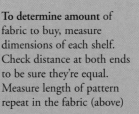

To determine amount of fabric to buy, measure dimensions of each shelf. Check distance at both ends to be sure they're equal. Measure length of pattern repeat in the fabric (above)

Buy enough fabric so the repeat starts at the top of each shelf (above). There will be some unused fabric—less with small pattern repeats. The fabric should be wide enough to fit the shelf.

Choosing Fabrics

• Line shelves with bed linens, tablecloths or curtain fabric to coordinate with other fabrics in the room.
• Use a tightly woven, opaque fabric that does not fray for the most satisfactory results. Loose weaves can shift out of shape when pasted.

• Heavy cotton fabrics work best with wallpaper paste; cotton-polyester blends are also suitable. Don't attempt to use paste with silk or other dry-cleanable fabrics.
• Look for patterns and colors that will complement, not overwhelm, display items.

Selecting Colors

• Darker prints highlight white display items nicely. Use light-colored fabrics to brighten up a dark shelf.
• Solid colors work best behind fine china or other delicate items. Look for

tone-on-tone textured fabrics (such as damask and brocade) to offset heirlooms.
• Make sure fabric colors are colorfast and will not bleed when wet.

Applying Fabric Shelf Lining

1 Measure exact shape of back of unit between shelves; check measurements at both ends. Add up to 4 inches in each direction for shrinkage; cut fabric. Make sure the pattern repeat is correctly placed.

2 Apply wallpaper paste to the back of the fabric, fold fabric over on itself and let it sit for 10 minutes to allow the fabric to absorb the wallpaper paste. Coat all of the fabric, especially the edges.

3 Open up one end of the fabric piece and spread it into place, aligning the upper edge of the fabric with shelf. Be careful not to pull on the fabric or stretch it out of shape; don't pull on the diagonal.

HANDY HINTS

If cupboard shelves are removable, take them out and work with one large piece of fabric to cover the entire back wall. Then replace the shelves when the fabric is dry.

DOLLAR SENSE

Wallpaper hanging kits usually include brushes, a seam roller and a razor knife in one handy, low-cost package. They are available at wallpaper and paint stores.

4 Finish spreading the fabric and smooth it into place with the smoothing brush. While paste is still moist, wipe off excess from the fabric and wood with a damp sponge. Use craft knife to trim any extra fabric from edges of shelf so that the fabric lies flat. Let dry.

FABRIC SHELVING SHADES

Decorative shades over shelves coordinate decor and neaten a room.

YOU WILL NEED

- ❏ MEASURING TAPE
- ❏ IRON
- ❏ DECORATOR FABRIC
- ❏ RING TAPE & CORDING
- ❏ HOOK-AND-LOOP TAPE
- ❏ WEIGHT ROD
- ❏ MOUNTING BOARD
- ❏ SEWING MACHINE
- ❏ SHEARS, THREAD & PINS
- ❏ STAPLE GUN
- ❏ SCREW EYES
- ❏ AWNING CLEATS

BEFORE YOU BEGIN

By using a coordinating fabric, a roller shade will become an integral part of the room's décor and not seem like a makeshift afterthought.

Fabric Considerations

Choose fabric that will coordinate with the rest of the room. If possible, match it to other fabric furnishings in the room, such as upholstery, window treatments or throw pillows.

For the best long lasting appearance, select a fairly heavyweight, closely woven fabric that will resist wrinkles and hold its shape well. The cloth should be opaque enough to conceal items on the shelves completely.

Good choices include heavy polished cotton, poplin, denim, canvas and sailcloth.

To determine the fabric measurements for the shade, measure the inside width

and length of the unit. Add 1 inch to the width and 5 inches to the length.

Before cutting the fabric, center the fabric's design so that the finished shade will not appear lopsided. If the shades will cover two adjacent units, center the overall design for a pleasing effect.

To attach the shade to the shelving unit, screw the mounting board at both ends to the top of the shelving unit, flush with the front edge (below).

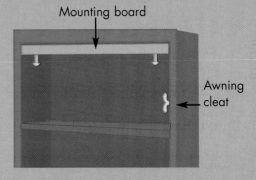

Mounting board

Awning cleat

Ring Tape Tips

- The number of rows of ring tape depends on the width of the fabric and the desired effect.
- Space the rows closely for a tailored shade; spread them out for softer folds.
- Run each cord up from the bottom ring, then

through the screw eyes at the top, leaving long ends hanging down one side for adjusting the shade.
- Trim the dangling ends even, braid and wind around an awning cleat to secure.

MAKING A FABRIC SHADE

1 Press under ½ inch on each long side of the fabric. Press under ½ inch at the bottom of the fabric; press under 3 inches again. Pin and stitch close to inner fold, leaving sides open. Press fabric under 1 inch at the top edge.

2 Cut hook-and-loop fastener tape equal to the fabric width measurement. Pin the loop side of the tape across the folded edge at the top of the fabric, covering the raw edge. Stitch the tape in place.

3 Making sure all the rings line up so that the shade will raise evenly, pin and stitch a length of ring tape to the back of the fabric at each side, covering the raw edges. Sew additional row(s) of ring tape in between.

4 Insert screw eyes into the top of the mounting board, with one screw eye aligned with each row of ring tape. Staple the hook side of the hook and loop fastener tape to the front of the mounting board.

5 Fasten the shade to the board, matching tapes. Tie a nylon cord to the bottom ring of each tape. Thread the cord up through the rings and across the mounting board to the right, through the screw eyes. Insert the weight rod in the pocket.

FITTED
TABLE COVER

Add a coordinating fitted cover to give a table a stylish, tailored finish.

BEFORE YOU BEGIN

Using a zigzag stitch, finish all the edges of each cut piece before making the table cover to minimize fraying during the project's construction.

Measuring and Cutting

A fitted table cover consists of a top joined to the skirt at the table edge.
• For the top, measure the top of the table; add ½ inch to all sides for seam allowance.

The skirt consists of a panel for each side of the table.
• For the length, measure the distance from the tabletop to the floor; add 2 inches. For the width, first plan the pleats.

Planning Pleats

Hold a piece of fabric up to the table and experiment with folds to determine the depth (a+b) and the width (c) of the pleat that looks best for the fabric.

Divide the width of the pleat (c) into each side measurement to determine the number of pleats per side. If the number attained contains a fraction, adjust the width of the pleat slightly to yield a whole number or plan to rearrange some of the pleats slightly so they fall evenly at the corners of the table.

To determine skirt panel width, multiply the number of pleats by $2(a + b) + c$; add 1 inch for seam allowances.

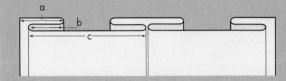

Allowing for Pattern Repeats

For a professional finish, match plaids and other fabrics with horizontal designs at the side seams.

To calculate the extra yardage required for matching side seams, measure the height of the pattern repeat. For each panel, add the size of the pattern repeat to the cut length required.

Begin by cutting the front panel. Then lay it beside the remaining yardage and align the pattern to determine where to cut the remaining three fabric panels.

MAKING A FITTED TABLE COVER

1 With right sides together, pin the skirt panels together, matching plaids. Beginning ½ inch down from the skirt's top edge, stitch the panels together with a ½-inch seam allowance. The seams should fall at the table corners.

2 Turn the fabric up 1½ inches along the bottom edge. For plaid fabric, follow a horizontal line to keep the hem straight; press and pin in place. Stitch the hem 1 inch away from the fold, then press the finished hem flat.

3 With the right side of the fabric facing up, form pleats in each skirt panel (Before you Begin). Plan the pleats so the panel seams fall at each corner of the tabletop; pin in place. Press folds from top to bottom.

HANDY HINTS

Choose heavy fabric and deep pleats for a formal appearance. Lighter fabric and gathers or unpressed pleats give a more casual impression.

OOPS

If a slight cutting error means that the plaids don't match exactly when the panel seams are pinned together, adjust the measurements. Compensate by trimming the resulting excess fabric from the panel that extends beyond the top and leaving less hem on that piece.

4 Once all the pleats have been pinned, machine-baste the pleats in place ½ inch from the top edge of the skirt; remove the pins. With right sides together, pin the top piece to the front panel of the skirt.

5 Stitch the top to the front skirt panel with a ½-inch seam allowance. Pivot at the corner then pin and stitch the next side. Repeat on the remaining two sides. Press the seams toward the cloth top. Turn the table cover right side out, touch up with the iron as necessary and fit onto the table.

FABRIC PATTERNS ADAPTED TO WALLS

Translate stylized motifs from linens to painted wall treatments.

YOU WILL NEED

- ❏ DECORATOR FABRIC
- ❏ TRACING PAPER
- ❏ RULER & LEVEL
- ❏ CRAFT KNIFE
- ❏ ACRYLIC PAINTS
- ❏ SMALL PAINTBRUSHES
- ❏ PAINTER'S MASKING TAPE
- ❏ PENCIL

BEFORE YOU BEGIN

Paint wall decorations that are inspired from favorite linens.

Create the Design

Place a sheet of tracing paper on top of the fabric design to be copied (below).

Choose the design elements to be included. A perfect imitation of the original is not at all necessary. Try to capture an eye-catching main motif and the mood of the fabric, whether it be whimsical, modern or elegant. Add enough details to bring depth to the rendering without making it busy.

Frame the motif if necessary by drawing a lined border around the design.

Make multiple photocopies of the simplified traced design on a photocopier, enlarging it as necessary to reach the desired size.

TRANSFERRING A FABRIC DESIGN

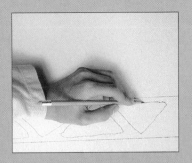

1 Using a level, mark the chair rail with a pencil, making it 2½ inches wide. Sketch triangles between the borders, alternating up and down points. Sketch a simple flower design inside the triangles.

2 To plot the arrangement of the motifs, measure the wall and then space horizontal and vertical rows so designs will be spread evenly. Mark a border framing the position of each motif placement.

3 On one photocopy (Before you Begin), cut out the main shape with a craft knife. Using painter's masking tape, secure the copy within the border on wall; trace design. Repeat in all borders.

HANDY HINTS

To keep the paint from smearing, start from the top, working down each column. Or, allow each color to dry thoroughly before applying the next one.

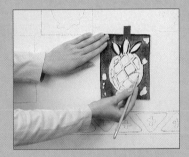

4 Using another photocopy of the complete design, cut out the motif's details with a craft knife. Sketch the details in place on the wall within the penciled border of each motif.

5 In every other column, paint the backgrounds within the borders as desired. For depth and variety, you may let the background of the second and fourth columns remain wall color. Fill in shapes for details with paint.

6 Using contrasting paint, add definition to the motif. With darker paint, add outlines and shadows. Paint the border with a coordinating dark paint.

7 Paint border lines of the chair rail using dark paint. Keep lines more or less straight without resorting to the rigid precision of painting against a ruler. Keep everything flowing and freehand to create a soft, whimsical effect.

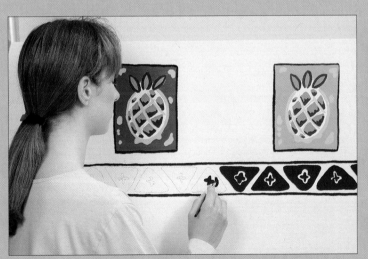

8 Once all other designs are completed, begin filling in the chair rail design. Using dark paint, paint in the chair rail's triangles and flower designs. Paint with a loose freehand style, but be sure that the dark paint conceals pencil outlines underneath. Allow designs to dry completely.

DISCOVER
SOLUTIONS

So many decorating projects come about because there is a challenge at hand. When there is such a challenge knocking at your door, there's no need to hide. All you need are a few ideas and then project instructions to carry them out. Chapters include:

- *Making Your View More Attractive*

- *Decorating Long and Narrow Rooms*

- *Uncovering Hidden Dining Possibilities*

MAKING YOUR VIEW MORE ATTRACTIVE

With a clever window disguise, you can hide an unpleasant outside view without blocking out the light.

MAKING IT WORK

This treatment is so appealing, you may want to use it in any sunny window—not just one with an unacceptable view!

Bright and Blooming

For a window that gets sunlight but looks out on a less-than-perfect view, shelves full of plants are ideal. Plants will love the direct light and you can enjoy the beauty of a **window green-house** (page 58).

• Fill the shelves full of blooms to conceal the view.

• Mix a variety of plants with different colors, textures and sizes to make the setting interesting.

• Glass shelves lighten up the overall feeling of the window area and allow a better view of the plants and their blooms.

• Use planters small enough to fit on shelves without crowding. Select a variety of planter shapes for extra interest.

• Outlining the window frame with a wallpaper border print or a **stenciled window border** (page 60) helps set off the window as a focal point.

VARIATIONS ON A THEME

Stained Glass

• A **stained glass panel** (page 62) allows light to filter in through the window while blocking out the scene on the other side.

• Look for details that tie the room elements together. The diamonds on the floor tiles echo the diamond design on the glass. The rose color in the glass is carried over to the wainscoting, paint, tiles and rug.

Antique Lace

• **Antique Linens** (page 64) complete the deceptively airy look of this window. The cafe curtain and valance let light stream in while concealing the view.

• Display pretty glass bottles and hide an unappealing outside view at the same time. Look for bottles in a variety of shapes and colors. Even the bottle stoppers look attractive.

FINISHING TOUCHES

Draw the eye away from a window's view by making the frame attractive and the inside elements bright and shiny.
• Use a decorative molding to frame the window.
• Paint the trim a color that matches the wall or one that picks up a color detail in the wallpaper.
• Accent the bright look of the molding with brass planters.
• For added interest, extend the wallpaper border around the room.

WINDOW GREENHOUSE

Create a view with foliage and blooms, and enjoy a stunning indoor garden.

YOU WILL NEED

- ❏ 1x6 WHITE PINE
- ❏ TAPE MEASURE
- ❏ PENCIL
- ❏ HAND DRILL & WOOD BORE DRILL BIT
- ❏ ⅜-INCH SISAL ROPE & ⅛-INCH TWINE
- ❏ SCREW EYES
- ❏ WOOD STAIN
- ❏ POLYURETHANE
- ❏ PAINTBRUSH
- ❏ FINE SANDPAPER
- ❏ GLUE GUN & GLUE STICKS
- ❏ LEVEL
- ❏ UTILITY SCISSORS

BEFORE YOU BEGIN

Match a wood stain to the existing window, or paint the shelf in a contrasting color.

Planning and Preparing

To determine the number of shelves and their sizes, measure the height (a), width (b) and depth (c) of the inside of the window casing. (See diagram below.)

• To determine the spacing between the shelves, measure the height of the potted plants and add 1 to 2 inches for "breathing room." A small window will accommodate two to three shelves. A large window looks more balanced with an odd number of shelves.

• From a 1x6, or narrower if necessary, piece of white pine or other soft wood, cut three shelves ¾ inch shorter than the width of the window. For a small charge, a lumberyard will precut the shelves.

• With fine-grade sandpaper, sand the top, bottom and ends of the wood shelves. Clean the surface using a soft cloth.

• Using utility scissors, cut four pieces of ⅜-inch natural sisal rope the height of the window opening, plus 25 inches—5 inches for each knot, plus 5 inches at each of the top and bottom shelves for looping through the screw eyes. Cut eight pieces of matching twine 30 inches long, to allow for wrapping the rope 12 times and for tucking the ends to secure.

• To prevent the wood from warping, place the vertical sisal supports every 30 inches or less to support the weight of the plants properly. For example, if a window measures more than 36 inches wide, add two ropes in the center of the window shelves and loop through the screw eyes.

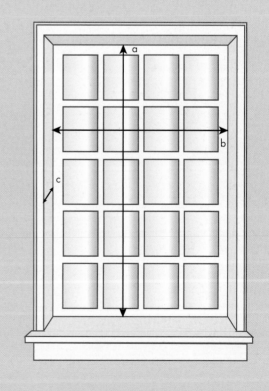

CRAFTING THE WINDOW GREENHOUSE

HANDY HINTS

A light stain is more attractive on soft wood. It stains the grain more evenly and prevents a mottled look. It also shows less soil.

TAKE NOTE

Make sure knots are tied at the same level so the shelf is balanced. Place a level on each shelf before moving to the next set of knots.

Place saucers under the pots to prevent water from spoiling the wood shelving.

1 Measure 3 inches from each end and 1 inch from the front and back edges of the shelves; mark with a pencil. Using a power drill and a ½-inch wood bore drill bit, drill four holes in each shelf. Finely sand the holes to smooth them.

2 Choose a stain to match or coordinate with the decor. With a foam brush, apply stain to the top, bottom and edges of the shelves. Lightly sand and reapply stain. Finish with a coat of polyurethane.

3 Starting at the bottom of the rope, take the distance from the sill to the first shelf, add 5 inches and tie knots. Slip the ropes up through the shelf holes. Repeat measuring and knotting for all the shelves, adding 5 inches at the top.

4 Drill holes in the top and bottom window casings 3⅜ inches in from the sides and 1 inch in from the front and back of the casing. Install screw eyes that are large enough for the sisal rope to slip through easily.

5 Put the rope ends through the top screw eyes. Loop the ropes down next to themselves for 5 inches. Knot twine around the sisal, then wrap tightly about 12 times around. Tuck the ends in and hot-glue to secure.

6 Carefully check the level of all the shelves and adjust the top knots, if necessary. Next, loop the ropes through the screw eyes up next to themselves at the bottom of the casing for 5 inches and repeat wrapping and securing with the twine. Glue the ends of all the wrapped ropes. Allow the ends to dry and then check that they are properly glued.

Stenciled Window Border

Highlight a window—not its view—by framing it with a brightly stenciled border.

YOU WILL NEED

- ❏ Border paint
- ❏ Paintbrushes
- ❏ Masking tape
- ❏ Stencil or acetate
- ❏ Stencil paint
- ❏ Stencil brushes
- ❏ Straightedge
- ❏ Scrap paper & pencil
- ❏ Paint trays
- ❏ Thick cardbord (if making stencil)

BEFORE YOU BEGIN

Stenciling around a window creates a focal point. For the brightest appearance, put a fresh coat of paint on the windows before doing the stenciling.

Planning the Stenciled Border

Plan the border and the positioning of the stencil.

• Using a straightedge and pencil, mark off the border area along the top and sides of the window and down to the baseboard.

• Make a mark at the center of the top of the window; then center the stencil design on that mark and lightly mark stencil placement. Continue to the left, then to the right, and down both sides.

• As an alternative, trace one complete stencil to the left side of the mark, then reverse the stencil and trace the pattern on the right side, continuing across the top and down the sides.

• Use a portion of the stencil to fill any leftover space in the corners if necessary.

• Draw both the border and the stencil pattern on a large sheet of craft paper if unsure how placement will look.

• Practice stenciling on scrap paper. Put a small amount of paint on the brush, dab excess on paper, and pounce, holding the brush vertically.

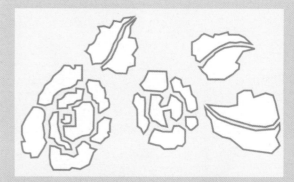

The design (above) is a simplified version of the rose stencil. To use it, enlarge it on a photocopier to the desired size. Trace the entire design on a piece of acetate. Or trace the stencil on two pieces of acetate, flower parts on one piece and leaves on the other. To transfer designs, place sheet of acetate on a thick cardboard surface. Use a craft knife to cut out the design elements. Change knife blades regularly to keep them sharp.

STENCILING THE BORDER

1 Place masking tape along the pencil lines for border. Apply two coats of paint, letting each dry. Do not remove the tape. Lightly mark the position of stencils around the window according to the plan.

2 Begin stenciling from the center top and then down the sides. On stencil, mask off leaves close to flowers. Tape the stencil in place. Dab brush in light pink paint and pounce on all of the flower's parts.

3 Do not move the stencil. Use a second brush to apply the darker pink to accent the flower along the petal edges. Or accent the petals from the center out. Let dry. Move stencil to next area.

HANDY HINTS

To be sure that the images stay clean, it is wise to buy two stencils in case the edges become rough or the stencil tears.

TAKE NOTE

If the brush is slanted while pouncing, bristles may go under the stencil edge, making the image fuzzy. Correct any mistakes by touching up with border paint once the stencil paint is dry.

4 When the pink is finished, clean the stencil well with warm water and soap while paint dries. Mask off flower parts very close to leaves on the stencil. Tape the stencil down to do the leaves, working from the top of the window and down the sides.

"Stained Glass" Panels

Blur an undesirable outside view with colorful panels of faux stained glass.

You Will Need

- ❑ Wooden frame
- ❑ Acrylic sheet
- ❑ Stained glass paint & leading
- ❑ Glazier's points
- ❑ Cup hooks
- ❑ Hammer
- ❑ Putty knife
- ❑ Drill & drill bit
- ❑ Ruler, black pen & pencil
- ❑ Foam board
- ❑ Utility knife

BEFORE YOU BEGIN

Substituting fragile glass panels with lightweight acrylic sheets ensures a stronger and more durable finished project.

Acrylic Sheets

Acrylic sheets make it easy to cut and design faux stained glass.

• Available at your local hardware store, ¼-inch-thick acrylic sheets are ideal for inserting into wooden frames.

• Cut the acrylic sheets to fit the selected frame by guiding a utility knife along the edge of a metal straightedge. Sheets thicker than ¼ inch must be cut by a professional.

Form and Frame

Enlarge the diamond pattern (*below*) to desired size on a photocopier or using graph paper. Position the design and trace it three times onto foam board or poster board that is the same size as the acrylic.

Many types of wooden frames with inside grooves along the back (custom, pre-assembled or snap-together) will work well with acrylic panels.

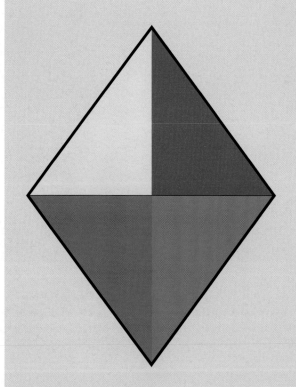

CRAFTING STAINED GLASS PANELS

OOPS

If the leading lines are crooked, carefully remove the leading from the acrylic with a utility knife and wipe clean with a cloth.

Lift paint spots from the acrylic by dipping a cotton swab into warm water and then gently rubbing it over the spot.

1 Referring to manufacturer's instructions, assemble the wooden frame. Use a hammer to tap the pieces together at the corners. If desired, add wood glue to the joints to secure.

2 Measure and mark the finished frame size on the paper side of the acrylic sheet, making sure the panel will fit into the grooves of the frame. Cut acrylic with a utility knife.

3 Transfer the stained glass pattern (Before you Begin) to foam board or poster board that is the same size as the acrylic sheet. Outline the design with a black pen for tracing.

4 Place the acrylic sheet over the foam board, aligning all sides; secure with tape. With the leading, carefully begin outlining the diamond pattern on the acrylic sheet; let dry, following manufacturer's instructions.

5 Beginning at the top, paint each section of the diamond with stained glass paint, allowing one color to dry (following manufacturer's instructions) before applying the next color. Keep the color placement consistent on each diamond; let dry.

6 For a textured effect, once the paint is dry, apply a clear crystal finish to the acrylic sheet on the background. Let the project cure at least a week before mounting it inside the frame.

7 Measure and mark the placement of the cup hooks along the top and bottom of the frames, 4 inches from each end. Drill a pilot hole at each mark, then tightly screw the cup hooks into the frame.

8 Place the stained glass inside the frame. Using a hammer and putty knife, lightly tap glazier's points around the back of the frame to secure the acrylic sheet. Attach cup hooks to the top of the window frame and hang.

WINDOW TREATMENTS FROM ANTIQUE LINENS

Transform pretty table linens into elegant window dressings.

BEFORE YOU BEGIN

With a little time and attention, and some planning, an embroidered or cutwork tablecloth can become a sensational window treatment.

Removing Spots

Remove stains or spots from old linens before working with them.

• Mildew and rust stains are also easily removed. Moisten the affected area with a lemon juice and salt mixture, then hang-dry the linens in the sun.

• For scorched areas on linen or cotton, dampen a cloth with a 3 percent hydrogen peroxide solution, commonly sold in drug stores as an antiseptic. Lay the dampened cloth on top of the scorched area and press it with a warm iron.

Measuring and Cutting Linens

For the final cut length, measure from the rod to the base of the window molding, or wherever you want the curtain to end. Add the circumference of the rod, plus 1 inch. (A hem allowance is not necessary since the linen's decorative edge will be the finished edge.)

• Finally, measure the width of the rod (right).

• Lay the tablecloth out on a large, flat surface so you can view the entire design to make best use of its decorative details.

• Measure the width and length of the cloth to ensure that it will fit the window with little adjustment (right).

• Cut one tablecloth in half lengthwise.

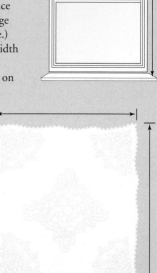

MAKING CURTAINS FROM TABLE LINENS

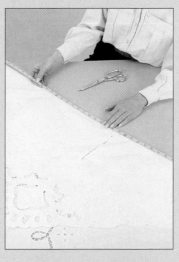

DOLLAR SENSE

Shop flea markets, auctions and estate sales for old table linens, handkerchiefs, dresser scarves and other antique linens for your projects.

QUICK FIX

Mend holes in old linens by embroidering around the raw edges of the hole with a buttonhole stitch. Match the embroidery floss to the fabric and incorporate the hole into the design.

1 With bias tape, finish side cut edge of each panel (Before you Begin). Open tape and match raw edges of tape and panel. Stitch together in fold of tape. Press tape to back; stitch close to folded edge of tape.

2 Measure finished width of each panel. On uncut tablecloth, fold decorative corner down at 45-degree angle until measurement of folded edge equals width of finished panel plus 1 inch. Cut along fold.

3 Pin right side of long edge of decorative triangle to wrong side of top edge of panel, matching edges. Stitch in place with ½-inch seam allowance. Press seam and turn triangle to right side of panel.

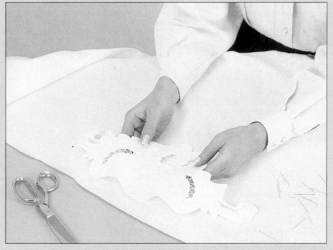

4 Using seam line as guide, mark down from top edge of panel the rod circumference plus 1 inch, for rod pocket. Stitch from top side along marks, creating rod pocket for decorative rod.

5 Cut out decorative motifs from remains of second tablecloth. Pin motifs to each curtain panel in center of panel side edge. Using short, narrow zigzag stitch and following detail lines of motif, stitch motif to each panel. Use sharp embroidery scissors and trim away open areas of motif from back, creating cutwork design on side edge of each panel. Hang panels on decorative rod.

DECORATING LONG AND NARROW ROOMS

Subtle decorating tricks help prevent tunnel vision in long and narrow rooms.

MAKING IT WORK

Tried and true decorating principles will transform a narrow "corridor" room into a comfortable retreat.

Casual Grouping

• Placing furniture at an angle de-emphasizes the room's boundaries. Group chairs around an ensemble of tables for a casual conversation area. Basic **wood furniture** (page 74) adds a subtle simplicity to the room.

• Keep accessories light and airy. Clean lines and minimal pillows keep the room from becoming cluttered.

• Painting the far wall a dark, shiny color appears to bring it closer. In turn, this visually raises the ceiling and makes the room seem wider. **Hanging wallpaper** (page 70) on the narrowest wall has the same effect.

• Stagger **shelving** (page 68) on the shorter walls to give an illusion of width. Vary size and height of items displayed on shelves for pleasing effect. Clear glass bottles and wire or mesh containers are attractive touches that don't take up much visual space.

• Wooden flooring laid on the diagonal or in a chevron will visually widen the room. A light neutral color on the floor makes the room appear larger.

VARIATIONS ON A THEME

Serene Slumber

• Pale colors on the walls, ceiling and trim reflect natural light, making the room appear wider. **Hanging wallpaper** (page 70) on the narrowest wall seems to bring it forward and widen the space.

• A monochromatic color scheme blends the furniture, walls and flooring together and prevents any one decorating element from dominating the space.

• Sheer curtains let maximum light flood into the room. When allowed to fall past the windowsill, the curtains help create an illusion of height.

Cozy Niche

• A round table and curvy, overstuffed chairs contrast with the corners and straight lines of the walls, windows and floor. Even the round lampshade lends a circular shape to the otherwise square room.

• A large mirror on a long wall catches light from the window and makes the room appear as if there are actually two windows. A metallic or **gilded frame** (page 72) also reflects the light.

• Break up the room into smaller functional areas to reduce the expanse of space visually.

WRAPPED IN COZY COMFORT

Long walls are ideal for displaying cherished family photographs in an interesting gallery format.
• Break the visual monotony of a long wall with frames in various shapes and colors.
• Create unity within the "gallery" by selecting frames made of the same materials.
• Arrange frames in an eclectic group, mixing and matching large and small frames.

MOLDING SHELVES FOR DISPLAYS

Molding makes a narrow shelf to show off your favorite collections.

BEFORE YOU BEGIN

Molding—normally considered an architectural detail—can be transformed into a functional and decorative shelf.

Cutting the Molding

Measure the area where the shelf will be hung to determine the lengths of molding needed. Using the plans below as guides, select moldings and small ⅜-inch-thick lumber. Take time to look at all the moldings available and trace the shapes to work out a plan similar to those below. To display collection pieces that take more room than upright plates, choose wider moldings and glue a wider piece of lumber to the top. All of the molding and lumber can be cut at the lumberyard to make the project even easier.

Three Different Molding Plans

Plan 1
This shelf has six components. A is a 1⅜-inch base molding trim. B and C are ⅜- by 2½-inch lumber. E is ⅜- by 4-inch lumber. D and F are both small cove moldings only ½- by ⅜-inch. All are available by the foot at lumberyards or occasionally in remnant pieces.

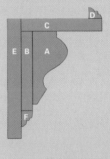

Plan 2
This shelf is a simplified version of the shelf in Plan 1. It's narrower but good for platters and plates. A is a standard chair rail. B and C are ⅜- by 3½-inch lumber. D is a small cove molding, ½- by ⅜-inch.

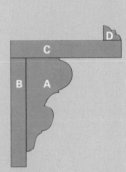

Plan 3
This shelf is very narrow and only big enough for small pieces. It uses the fewest pieces. A is a 2¼ inch solid crown molding. B is ⅜- by 2½-inch lumber. C is small cove molding, ½- by ⅜-inch.

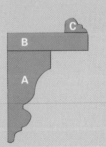

ASSEMBLING A MOLDING SHELF

1 Referring to Plan 1, glue molding (A) to smaller backing piece (B) with top edges even. Then glue small cove molding (D) to top (C). Apply wood glue to one surface, press pieces together. Hammer in nails; let glue dry.

2 When A/B and C/D have dried, glue them together. Apply the glue to the top of A/B and press to C/D firmly. Make sure the back surfaces are flush and the ends are even before the glue becomes tacky.

3 After glue has dried, glue large back piece (E) to backs of B and C. Apply glue to both B and C. Apply glue to both B and C in streaks across area and close to edges. Press onto E and adjust the top for a flush surface and even ends.

HANDY HINTS

Because the quality and color of wood molding varies, it is best to paint rather than stain these molding shelves. Painting will unify the separate parts.

TAKE NOTE

Use nails to ensure the pieces of wood will stay firmly together while the glue dries. C clamps can also be used to hold the wood pieces together.

4 Let the glue dry completely. To attach the small cove molding (F), apply glue to two flat surfaces of F and fit into the right angle surfaces of B and E. Adjust the ends until they are even and let dry.

5 Lightly sand the ends of the assembled shelf. Apply a generous layer of wood putty to fill in the openings between moldings. Let dry for several hours. Sand with fine sandpaper until the wood fill is smooth.

6 Apply one coat of primer and let it dry. Then paint the shelf with one or two coats for a good cover. Hammer the hangers on the back of the shelf, placing one at each end at the top edge.

WALLPAPER TO ACCENT ONE WALL

Patterned wallpaper creates the illusion of a closer, wider wall in narrow space.

YOU WILL NEED

- ❏ TAPE MEASURE
- ❏ WALLPAPER
- ❏ WALLPAPER PASTE
- ❏ PASTING BRUSH
- ❏ LEVEL & CHALK
- ❏ SEAM ROLLER
- ❏ SPREADING BRUSH
- ❏ DAMP SPONGE
- ❏ RAZOR KNIFE
- ❏ WIDE PUTTY KNIFE

BEFORE YOU BEGIN

Hold up the wallpaper to check the pattern before cutting. Place the top edge of repeat at the top of wall.

Determining the Amount

- Wallpaper with no pattern or a random repeat is easy to calculate. Simply multiply height by the width of the wall.
- For wallpaper with a repeat, measure distance from start of one pattern to start of next. Divide the wall height (in inches) by the inches between repeats and round up. Then multiply this number by distance between repeats to get the working height. Now multiply working height by wall width.

Cutting Wallpaper Strips

Plan for a full pattern design to fall below the ceiling. Add 2 inches above that, and cut top edge of strip. From top of cut edge, measure wall height, adding 4 inches. Cut bottom of strip. Cut the rest of the strips one at a time so each is long enough for patterns to match at joins.

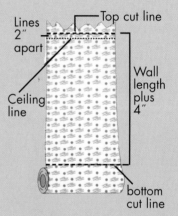

Lines 2" apart

Top cut line

Ceiling line

Wall length plus 4"

bottom cut line

Pasting the Wallpaper

Brush on paste and fold both ends of strip into middle (*right*), aligning edges. Do not overlap ends or crease folds. Roll loosely. Let sit for 10 minutes before hanging. This technique is called booking; it gives the wallpaper time to absorb paste and relax to its original shape.

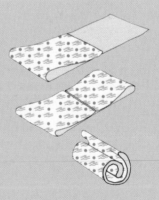

PUTTING UP WALLPAPER

1 Lay the wallpaper out on a large, clean work surface. Paste first strip according to manufacturer's directions. Book the strip (Before you Begin).

2 At intervals, measure from corner the width of wallpaper and connect marks with chalk. Check with a level to be sure line is a true vertical.

3 Unfold top section of first strip and position paper at ceiling line, overlapping by 2 inches. Press strip to wall so edge is next to the vertical chalk line.

4 Unfold remaining section of first strip; press into place without stretching. Adjust placement, as necessary, using vertical chalk line as a guide.

5 Smooth with brush, fanning out from the center. Remove all the air bubbles and make certain the wallpaper is securely pasted to the wall.

6 Run seam roller along side edges of wallpaper to ensure that seams are flat and secure. Wipe off the excess adhesive with a damp sponge.

7 Use razor knife and wide putty knife to cut upper and lower edges of wallpaper. Do this on side edge if paper extends around corner.

8 Wipe off entire wallpaper surface, baseboards and edge of ceiling with damp sponge. Make sure to remove excess adhesive. Rinse sponge often.

9 Hang second piece. Butt edges and make sure pattern is aligned with first piece. Ease into place without stretching. Repeat Steps 4 through 8.

HANDY HINTS

Use primer on the walls before hanging the wallpaper. The paper will adhere more readily to the wall and color won't bleed through.

Wallpaper hanging kits usually include brushes, a seam roller and a razor knife in one handy, low-cost package. They are available at wallpaper and paint stores.

TAKE NOTE

Prepasted vinyl wallpaper is usually easier to work with than regular paper. Consider using it for your first project.

DOLLAR SENSE

Wallpaper is sold in dye lots and can be hard to match at a later date. Buy extra if uncertain about the amount needed.

GILDED PICTURE FRAMES

Gilded frames can reflect light and brighten small spaces, making them appear larger.

YOU WILL NEED

- ❏ MINERAL SPIRITS
- ❏ FINE SANDPAPER
- ❏ WOODEN FRAME
- ❏ BLACK OR RED ENAMEL PAINT
- ❏ GOLD ACRYLIC PAINT
- ❏ ARTIST'S BROWN OIL PAINT (SUCH AS BURNT UMBER)
- ❏ PAINT GLAZE
- ❏ PAINTBRUSHES
- ❏ HAIR DRYER
- ❏ COTTON CLOTH
- ❏ SMALL CAN FOR MIXING

BEFORE YOU BEGIN

Create antique or modern effects with the right combination of base coat, gold paint and shading colors. Practice the technique before starting.

Picking Paints and Frames

The shape of the frame and the paints you choose will affect the final result.
• For an antique effect, use black or red enamel paint as a base coat to give extra depth of color to the gold finishing paint. Don't worry if the gold paint does not take very well to the shiny base coat.

• Gold metallic paint is an acrylic water-based paint, available in small quantities. Light and dark gold were used on these frames, but other tones and textures are available.
• Give the gold finish an aged look with a coat of paint glaze, tinted with a little artist's oil paint.

Picture frames (*right*) should have a raised pattern to best show off the gilding effect. Choose either wooden frames with deep moldings or more elaborate frames, such as ones with raised flowers and beading. The paint highlights the raised parts of the pattern and creates a classic look.

Remove the backing, picture and glass from the frame before starting the process (*right*). Then, wipe the frame with a cloth soaked in mineral spirits to remove any grease or polish on the frame. Finally, rub the frame down with very fine sandpaper to create a smooth working surface.

PAINTING A FRAME

HANDY HINTS

For an evenly tinted paint glaze, first mix artist's oil paint with an equal quantity of mineral spirits. Then, gradually blend in the paint glaze to achieve the desired tint. This method creates a smoother blend than if you just drop the oil paint into the glaze.

1 First prepare the frame (Before you Begin). Then use a narrow brush that is fine enough to work the paint into the molded shape of the frame. Apply an even coat of black or red enamel paint. This gives a smooth, glossy base to build up further layers of color.

2 When the base is dry, use a clean brush to apply a coat of light gold paint. This can be applied liberally—a perfect finish is not necessary, and imperfections will help to give the frame an antique look.

3 As soon as the gold is applied, use a hair dryer to distress the frame. The heat from the dryer makes the gold paint crack and bubble so that some of the base coat shows through.

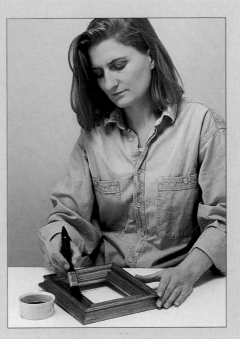

4 Thin the dark gold paint with mineral spirits, mixing about one part of mineral spirits to three parts of paint. Apply the mixture liberally over the frame so that it runs into the moldings and any cracks in the surface.

5 Before the paint dries, dampen a clean, lint-free cotton cloth with mineral spirits. Wipe the entire surface of the frame with the cloth, lifting off most of the dark gold paint, except in the cracks.

6 Finally, apply a protective finish to the frame with a coat of paint glaze. To enhance the antique effect, tint the glaze with artist's oil paint in a brown tone such as burnt umber. Apply the tinted glaze evenly to the frame. Then let it dry in a dust-free location.

PICKLED WOOD FURNITURE

Brighten and soften wood grain furniture with this easy finishing technique.

BEFORE YOU BEGIN

Pickled wood has a subtle, grainy appearance. The technique can enhance furniture, wall paneling, wood boxes and small wood objects.

Pickling Preparation

Pickling works best on unfinished, open-grain wood such as pine, oak and ash (above).

If you want to pickle an old wood surface, first use a commercial wood stripper to completely remove all of the old paint. A wire brush (below) can help remove old finish from crevices and carved areas.

Prior to being pickled, new or stripped furniture must be sanded smooth:
• Rub the furniture with successively finer grades of sandpaper (below left).
• Always sand in the direction of the wood grain.
• Use a sanding block, available at hardware stores.
• For spindles, crevices and other curved or hard-to-reach areas, use fine steel wool (below right).
• Remove all dust with a tack cloth or vacuum cleaner.

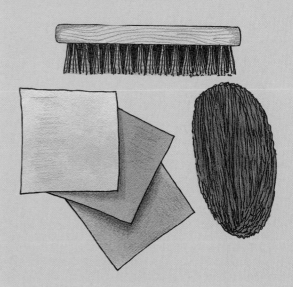

Pickling Pointers

• For the pickling mixture, dilute one part latex paint with between one and ten parts water. Test the mixture on an inconspicuous spot. Add more water, if necessary, to achieve the desired look.

• Do not stop pickling midway through a surface or there will be a line of deeper color where the wet and dry mixtures meet.

PICKLING A ROCKING CHAIR

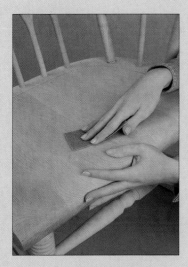

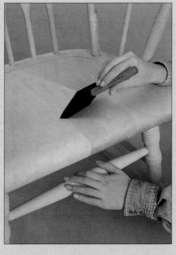

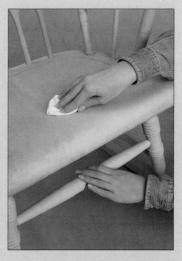

TAKE NOTE

Oil-based varnishes tend to yellow with time, which means they are not appropriate for white pickled wood projects.

1 Using 400-grit sandpaper, sand the rocking chair lightly in the direction of the wood grain. In a plastic plate or paint tray, mix the paint (Before you Begin) with enough water to create a light cream consistency.

2 Using a foam brush, apply a liberal amount of the diluted paint or "pickling mix" to the chair. Work on one section at a time, but be sure to complete the entire surface before the paint has dried.

3 For a light pickled effect, wipe off the paint mixture with a lint-free cloth. For a darker pickled effect, let the paint mixture remain on the wood for about five minutes before you wipe it off.

4 Let the pickling mixture dry thoroughly. If you want more grain to show through, sand the chair lightly. Apply two coats of water-based varnish to the surface of the chair; allow each coat of varnish to dry completely.

UNCOVERING HIDDEN DINING POSSIBILITIES

Make room for dinner guests no matter how small your living and dining space.

MAKING IT WORK

Turning a coffee table into dining space is an easy and inexpensive switch, especially when all the necessary parts are within easy reach.

Double Duty Furniture

This cleverly arranged living room doubles as a dining area when guests come and a few extra place settings are needed.

• A chest of drawers is a convenient storage place for table linens, cutlery and **napkin rings** (page 94). It holds more than the average sideboard and fits the low look of this table and the cushions.

• **Place mats** (pages 84, 86, 88) or **linens** (pages 78, 80, 82, 96) that coordinate with the patterns in the room make the transformation to dining look planned.

• Large floor cushions easily convert to table seating. Oversized cushions guarantee that both dining and reclining will be comfortable.

VARIATIONS ON A THEME

Converting an Office Space

• Any flat work surface, including a desktop like this one, can serve as a sideboard table for a buffet dinner.

• When extra space is needed for dining, stow all the computer equipment and desk supplies on the floor, cleverly tucked behind the floor-length covering.

• First cover the desk with a full-lenghth, light-colored rectangular **tablecloth** (pages 90, 92) or one that matches the wall and blends in well with the surroundings. Then top it with a darker, shorter tablecloth, either placed over the first cloth at an angle or tied up at all four corners for a soft, swagged look.

COORDINATING TABLEWARE

No matter where you set a table, the tableware helps set the tone—from casual to formal.
• Gather napkins in decorative rings to add color that coordinates with the setting.
• Use similar soft colors for a casual but coordinated tabletop look.
• Mix and match china and crystal to create unique combinations.
• Look for discontinued pieces at bargain prices for accents.

Transformed Card Table

Use an easy-to-make table cover to disguise utilitarian furniture.

BEFORE YOU BEGIN

The type of fabric or pattern you choose will determine the look of the table. A bright plaid looks casual while a silky jacquard says elegant.

Determining Fabric Yardage

To create fitted sides that are easy to sew, this tablecloth is made up of three pieces. Determine overall dimensions:

Measure size of table top (A); add 1 inch for hems.

Determine drop of cloth (B); about 8" is good; add 1 inch for hems.

Dimensions of large piece:
• Height = A + 2B
• Width = A

Dimensions of small piece:
• Height = A
• Width = B
• Note dimensions and tablecloth piecing on a sample layout.

Add all width measurements together. If the total is less than the width of the fabric you want, purchase yardage equal to the height of the largest piece.

Add yardage if you plan to make chair covers and welting. To calculate, add together the height of the chair back plus 1 inch plus ½ yard (for the welting).

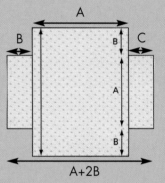

Chair Cover

Make a pattern of the chair back shape to make this job easy.
• Trace the chair back onto a piece of paper.
• Add ½ inch all around for seams; add ½ inch to account for depth.
• Cut two pieces of fabric from pattern.

• Sew welting to right side of one piece along rounded edge, starting and stopping ½ inch from ends (do not cut ends of welting). Sew both pieces right sides together. Turn up lower edge twice, ¼ inch; press and stitch.

Sewing Instructions

All seam allowances when sewing home decorating projects are ½ inch, unless stated otherwise.

Sewing the Tablecloth

HANDY HINTS

For more information about welting, see page 102.

TAKE NOTE

If you are using a plaid fabric, or one with a definite repeat, it is important to match the placement of the side panels to the area on the tabletop pattern piece with which they align. Purchase extra fabric to match patterns.

1 Fold each short edge of the tablecloth (top and bottom edges) 8½ inches to wrong side; pin in place and press. Along one long edge of each side panel, place a pin marking ½ inch in from each of the short edges.

2 With right sides facing, pin the long edges of the side panels to the long edges of the large tablecloth piece, matching pin markings to pressing lines. Stitch together between the pin marks, securing ends.

3 Trim seam allowances and press seams toward short panels. Pin panel short side edges to drop of large piece (the part of the large tablecloth piece extending beyond the 8½-inch press mark); stitch in place.

4 Clip the corner edges and trim the seams. Fold the entire hem edge of the completed tablecloth ½ inch to the wrong side and press. Topstitch ¼ inch from pressed edge. If the fabric has a tendency to fray, fold the ends under ¼ inch then ¼ inch again; press and stitch.

SIMPLE SLIPCOVERS FOR FOLDING CHAIRS

Dress up an ordinary folding chair with an elegant slipcover.

BEFORE YOU BEGIN

For the pattern pieces, cover the chair, one section at a time, with tissue paper. Transfer all markings to the tissue paper. Include ½-inch seam allowances on all sides.

Making a Pattern

Chair seat/front. Form darts (6½ inches wide at the base and 5½ inches long) at each side of the seat fold to help make an "L" shape for the seat when stitched. Mark the front corners for pleat placement.

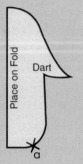

Chair sides. Trace the chair side shape, starting at the back edge and continuing to the front seat corners. Add 3½ inches to the front edge for the pleat and 2 inches to the length for a hem.

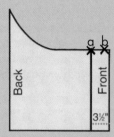

Back. Mark half the back on the tissue. Make one mark 6¾ inches from the top edge of the center back; another 3¼ inches from the center at the bottom; connect the marks. Add 2 inches to the length all around for the hem.

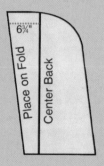

Chair front panel. Mark a rectangle as wide as the chair front, plus 10 inches for pleats and seam allowance, and as high as the distance between the seat and the floor, plus 2½ inches.

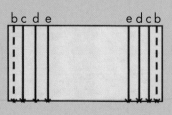

Fabric Layout and Cutting

One slipcover requires about 2¼ yards of 54-inch-wide fabric. You will need more for narrower fabric widths or to match patterns.

To cut fabric, make sure all pattern pieces run in the same direction. For front and back pieces, place patterns on folded fabric.

Sewing a Slipcover for a Chair

1 Pin the side pieces of the slip-cover to the back with the right sides together and the bottom edges of the fabric even. Stitch the slipcover pieces together with a ½-inch seam.

2 To make the back pleat, fold the back, right sides together, matching the pattern's solid lines. Pin and stitch along the solid line from the top down 10 inches. Baste from that point to the bottom.

3 Form the slipcover's center back pleat by aligning the center back fold and the seam line. Baste across the upper edge of the pleat to hold it in place. Press the pleat.

4 With right sides together, pin the front panel to the side pieces and stitch with a ½-inch seam. Form the corner pleats by folding the fabric along "b" and "d" so that "a" and "e" meet "c."

5 Pin the fabric, right sides together, at the back corners of the seat fabric as indicated on the pattern pieces to form a dart. Pin and stitch the dart in place.

6 Pin the piping to the right side of the chair seat/front piece, having raw edges even. Allow 1 inch extra of cording for joining. Baste along the seam line.

7 Pin baste and stitch the front to the back, right sides together and sandwiching piping. Press the hem under ½ inch, then 1½ inches; stitch in place along inner fold.

8 Stitch two pairs of buttons to the chair back. Sew two narrow fabric loops. Twist a loop around each button pair.

No-Sew Slipcovers

Perfect for a party or to add punch to plain chairs, these cover-ups are simple to make.

YOU WILL NEED

- ❏ DECORATIVE FABRIC
  OR TABLECLOTH
- ❏ FUSIBLE LAMINATE
- ❏ 1-INCH GROSGRAIN
  RIBBON
- ❏ HOLE PUNCH
- ❏ SHEARS
- ❏ PENCIL
- ❏ BOWL OR GLASS
- ❏ TAPE MEASURE
- ❏ IRON

BEFORE YOU BEGIN

The key to a perfectly fitted slipcover is careful measuring. Keep in mind that it is better for a slipcover to be a little large instead of too small.

Cutting the Laminating Fabric

- For extra protection against party spills and stains, laminate the fabric. Lightweight fabrics work well, but you can also laminate heavier, lined fabrics.
- Follow manufacturer's instructions to laminate fabrics, after removing any loose particles from the fabric surface.
- For the skirt's side flaps, measure the distance (a) from the floor, to the seat edge, across the width of the seat and down to the floor. Add ½ inch for ease. Measure the depth of the seat.
- For the front and back flaps, measure (b) from the floor to the seat edge, across the depth of the seat and to the floor again. Add ½ inch for ease. Measure the seat width.
- For a short skirt, start and end your measurements at the point on the chair leg where you'd like the slipcover to stop.
- Transfer the measurements to your fabric to create the cross-shaped slipcover (below), making sure the side flaps are as wide as the seat depth and the front and back flaps are as wide as the seat width.

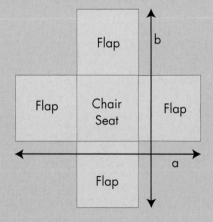

Design Ideas

The design options for slipcovers are limitless.
- For holiday decorating, cut slipcovers from seasonal fabrics.
- Instead of scalloping the edges, cut zigzags, or cut one large curve for each side flap.
- Hot-glue a pretty trim, such as pom-pom or fringe, around the edges of the slipcover.
- Substitute cording or rope for the ribbons.

MAKING A NO-SEW COVER

1 Lay the fabric on a flat surface with pattern markings facing up. Cut out seat cover with scissors, keeping lines straight and even. Repeat to cut out slipcovers for remaining chairs.

2 Measure 2 inches down from top of side flap and ¾ inch in from outside edge of side flap. Repeat on back flap. Lightly mark for ribbon hole placement. Repeat marking for ribbons on corners. Punch out holes at markings.

3 To create scalloped edges, position small bowl or glass along edge of side flaps. Using pencil, trace around curve of bowl; lift bowl and draw another curve. Continue until scalloped pattern forms; cut out.

4 Position slipcover over chair so all flaps are aligned along bottom. Cut four pieces of ribbon, 15 inches long, for each chair. Thread ribbon through hole on one flap and out hole on adjacent flap. Tie into bow, then trim ends diagonally. Repeat for all ribbons.

HANDY HINTS

Instead of laminating decorative fabric, cut slipcovers from tablecloths made from pre-laminated or plastic-coated fabrics.

You can also use regular (nonlaminated) fabric to make the slipcovers. Finish the raw edges with fusible tape.

Rather than punching holes for ribbons, add grommets. For information about working with grommets, see pages 156 and 157.

OOPS

If the punched hole pulls through to the edge of the fabric, remove the slipcover from the chair. Fuse a lightweight patch to the back of the slipcover over the hole, then repunch the hole.

If the flaps are different lengths when the slipcover is in place, trim the bottom edges even with one another.

BORDERED PLACE MATS

Set an inviting table with bordered place mats created to match your theme or decor.

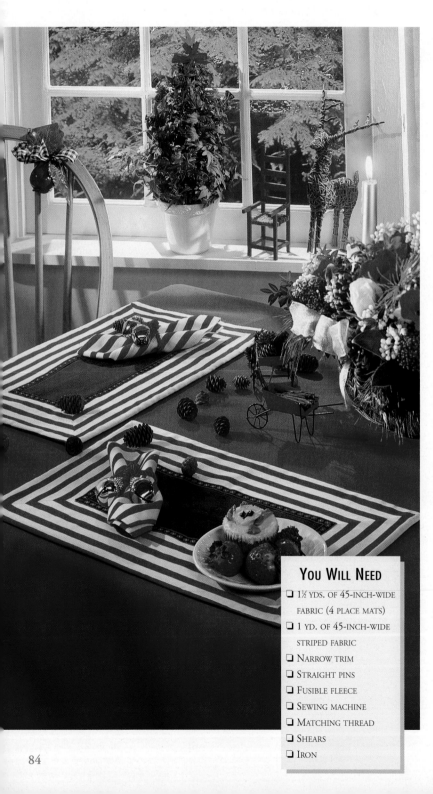

BEFORE YOU BEGIN

Create a custom look for your place settings with bordered place mats.

Cutting the Fabric

- For the top and bottom of each place mat, cut two rectangles, 18½ inches by 12½ inches, from solid-colored fabric.
- For the striped, mitered border, cut two 3½-inch-wide fabric strips 34 inches long for each place mat.
- Cut one piece of fusible fleece 18½ inches by 12½ inches for each place mat. All seam allowances will be ½ inch.
- Following manufacturer's instructions, fuse fleece to the wrong side of each place mat bottom piece. The fleece will provide a cushion between the place mat and the tabletop.

Working with Stripes

Careful planning before cutting a striped border is very important: Make sure each edge starts with the same color of stripe. With stripes running the length of the 3½-inch-wide strips, place two strips right sides together, matching stripes. The 45° angle creates a traditional mitered border.

For a different look, cut the 3½-inch-wide border strips so the stripes run up and down the depth of the strips. Place two strips right sides together, matching stripes of the same color. The 45° angle creates a herringbone effect in each corner.

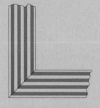 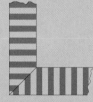

Prequilted Place Mat

Prequilted fabric adds texture to the center section of these place mats. Layer quilted fabric on the top and bottom to offer added protection for the table surface.

- Cut a 4-inch border out of a fresh, pretty chintz. If the print allows, match the design at the corners.

- Topstitch the inside border edge with matching thread to hold the border fabric in position.

MAKING BORDERED PLACE MATS

HANDY HINTS

Make reversible place mats by using different but coordinated fabrics for the top, bottom and border pieces.

1 Baste together wrong sides of place mat top and fleece-backed bottom. Press in ¼ inch on one edge of border strips. Right sides together, with ½ inch of strip extending beyond mat, pin raw edge of strip to bottom of mat.

2 Using ½ inch seam allowance, stitch first strip to mat beginning and ending ½ inch in from corners. Cut excess fabric so ½ inch of strip extends at end. Stitch strips to remaining three sides same way. Open strip ends.

3 Fold back open strip ends diagonally and crease them. Place corner fabric strips right sides together and stitch in crease line creating mitered corners. Clip corners. Trim and press open seam allowances.

4 Complete stitching all corners along outer edge. Turn border over to top side of mat, encasing seam allowance. Trim corners again, if necessary. Press border fabric flat.

5 Pin border fabric in place to avoid slippage while topstitching. Match top and bobbin threads to fabric color, then topstitch close to inside pressed edge. Beginning at one corner, center trim over topstitching and stitch through all layers along inner edge. For corners, fold trim at 90° angle and continue stitching. At end, turn trim back ¼ inch and overlap edge; stitch. Stitch along outer edge to finish.

Place Mats for a Round Table

Create customized place mats that fit your table—and your decor—perfectly.

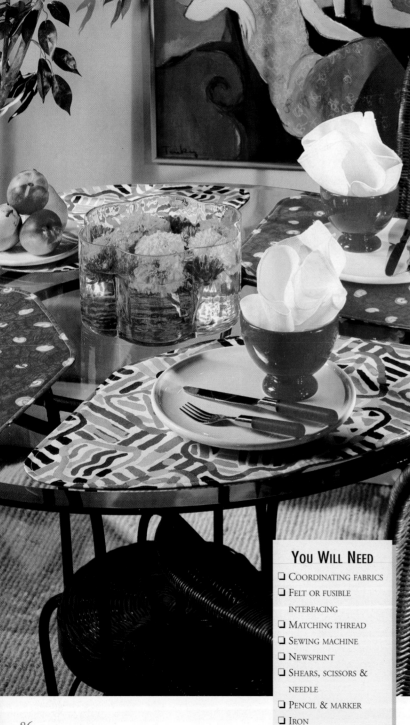

BEFORE YOU BEGIN

Reversible, shaped place mats, custom-stitched to fit the size of your tabletop, eliminate the problem of corners hanging over the edge of a round table.

Making a Place Mat Pattern

To determine correct place mat size, lay newsprint on top of table. Trace top; cut out.

• Fold newsprint in half twice to make four place mats; fold in half three times for eight mats. Cut newsprint along fold lines. For odd number of mats, divide perimeter of table by the number of mats needed. Mark off this measurement around edge of circle. Connect each mark to center of circle to form pie shapes; cut out.

• On a pie shape, mark down 6½ inches on each side from top point. Connect the two points. Cut point off along this line. Cut off 1 inch on curved edge.

• Fold pattern in half lengthwise. Mark in ¼ inch from side edges; cut on mark. Use edge of bowl to mark curves at top and bottom corners. Cut out pattern on markings.

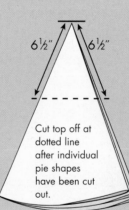

Cut top off at dotted line after individual pie shapes have been cut out.

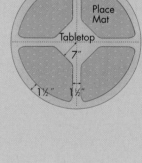

Table Tips

To protect the table surface from heat, interface the place mats with felt instead of fusible interfacing.

• A heat-resistant fabric can be used as an interfacing. Baste the fabric to the wrong side of the back of the place mat, then stitch the front and back pieces together.

• To accent the place mats, add pretty trims around the outside edges, or stitch decorative piping between the seamlines.

MAKING SHAPED PLACE MATS

HANDY HINTS

To protect the fabric, apply an iron-on laminate to the front of the fabric before cutting out the place mats. Iron-on laminate can be purchased at craft shops and fabric stores.

1 Place pattern on wrong side of fabric; centering over fabric design, if necessary. Trace and cut out desired number of mats. For reverse side of mats, place pattern on contrasting fabric and cut out.

2 Using mat pattern cut two fusible interfacing pieces for each mat; fuse to wrong side of each fabric. With right sides facing and raw edges even, stitch mats together; leave 4- to 6-inch opening for turning.

3 Clip curves and trim seams, making one seam allowance narrower than the other. Turn each place mat right side out. To define curves, use small point of scissors to carefully push fabric toward seamline. Press seams flat with warm iron.

TAKE NOTE

Prewash fabrics before stitching. This removes sizing and prevents place mats from shrinking during subsequent washings.

4 Press raw edges in opening to inside of place mat and pin in place. Working on back side of place mat, slipstitch the opening closed with matching thread. Using warm iron, press flat.

5 With matching thread, topstitch around edges of each place mat, ¼ inch from outside edge. Clip threads at ends of seam. When all place mats are finished, position them on table so curved edges fall 1½ inch in from edge of tabletop.

STENCILED PLACE MATS

Stenciled cork place mats add texture and dimension to your place settings.

YOU WILL NEED

❏ CORK PLACE MATS
❏ STENCILS
❏ ARTIST'S ACRYLIC PAINT
❏ ARTIST'S OR STENCIL BRUSHES
❏ PLASTIC LID OR PLATE
❏ SCISSORS & SCRAP PAPER
❏ COLORED PENCILS & CRAYONS
❏ PAPER TOWELS
❏ MASKING TAPE

BEFORE YOU BEGIN

Plan the design with cutouts of the whole shape. Reposition until the pattern is pleasing. Large items can be centered or placed asymmetrically.

Planning the Design

Trace each of the stencil shapes on scrap paper with a pencil. Select colors that blend with each other and contrast with the background. Color in shapes using crayons or colored pencils.

Cut out decorative items in whole units as well as in separate parts. This makes it easy to see one complete design as well as how the separate parts of the design will look when repeated several times.

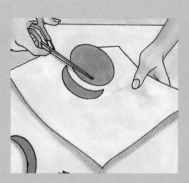

Position the paper shapes on the place mat. Rearrange shapes or change colors until satisfied with the placement. Before making a final decision, experiment with plate and napkin placement.

Practicing Painting

Practice using the right amount of paint and the proper brush stroke to ensure stenciling success.
• Pour a small amount of paint onto a large plastic lid or a plastic plate.
• On several layers of paper towels, dab and swirl brush to blend paint into bristles and remove most of the excess paint.
• Practice brushing in a spiral fashion, starting at outer edge of stencil and brushing toward center of design.

STENCILING PLACE MATS

OOPS

Mask off the cutouts planned for other colors to prevent painting by mistake.

Camouflage any drips or bleeding by touching up with paint that matches the background of the place mat.

1 Cut scrap paper to mat size and trace stencil design following placement of paper cutouts. Test color and paint absorption on back of placemat. Following paper layout, position and tape largest design.

2 Dip brush into selected paint and swirl on paper towels to remove excess. Paint the first design area. Be sure paint doesn't seep under stencil. Let dry before removing stencil. Complete one color at a time.

3 Position and tape second color area. Paint using a new brush or clean, completely dry brush. Position stencil carefully when applying second color so patterns align or overlap as appropriate.

4 Let the second paint color dry thoroughly. Use a new brush or a washed and dried brush to apply the last paint color. For an added touch, select a portion of the design to accent and coordinate the corners of cloth napkins.

RIBBON TABLECLOTH

Use pretty ribbon to customize a tablecloth, then tie extra ribbon around napkins.

BEFORE YOU BEGIN

Adding ribbons to a ready-made tablecloth gives it extra pizzazz. If you can't find a suitable tablecloth, you can always make one yourself.

Buying Ribbons

For this project, polyester ribbons are ideal.
- Choose fully washable, woven-edge ribbons.
- Polyester ribbons can be stitched to either synthetic or natural fabrics.
- Double satin gives a luxurious finish.
- Use a multipurpose polyester thread that matches the ribbon.

Choosing Tablecloth or Fabric

The tablecloth must be square if you want it to lay diagonally on the table as shown here.
- Cotton or linen cloths should be pre-shrunk.
- Wash deep-colored cloths several times in cold water so dye from the cloth will not discolor the ribbons.
- To avoid seams, choose fabric wide enough to cover the entire table.
- For large tables, sheeting fabric is suitable and is available in a variety of dark, rich colors.
- Check that the corners of the fabric are true right angles by aligning each with the corner of a square or rectangular table.
- Machine stitch hems, or hem or slipstitch by hand (below) for an elegant edge.

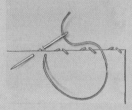

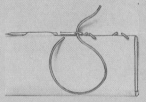

A hemming stitch is done with small, slanted stitches. Pick up just a couple of threads with each stitch.

Slipstitching is less visible than hemming, but it is not as strong. Slip the needle further through the fabric of the hem.

ADDING RIBBONS TO A TABLECLOTH

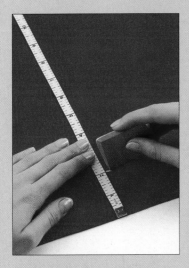

QUICK FIX

If you are confident with your sewing machine and the cloth is not too slippery, you can save basting time by simply pinning the ribbons in place. Position the pins across the ribbons removing them just before stitching the ribbon in place.

1 Decide exactly where the ribbons will go on the tablecloth. Use a tape measure to check the spacing, and make a series of marks using tailor's chalk.

2 Join the marks using a yardstick or ruler. In the display example, there are two rows of ribbons. The 1-inch-wide ribbon is placed 2 inches from the edge of the cloth and the ½-inch-wide ribbon is 3½ inches from the edge.

3 Pin the ribbons in place so they just cover the chalk line. To prevent waste, do not cut the ribbon until completing one edge of the cloth. This way, you will use only the exact amount needed.

DOLLAR SENSE

Make the most of old or damaged tablecloths by covering any stains or small holes with ribbon. Choose ribbon widths depending on size of area to be covered, and don't limit placement to the edge of the cloth. Try diamond-shaped ribbon patterns over the center of the tablecloth if necessary.

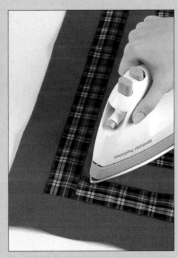

4 Baste or pin the ribbons in place, leaving the ends free. At the corners, cut one ribbon longer than the other so that it can be turned under neatly to enclose raw edges. Baste or pin the ends of the ribbons in place.

5 When all the ribbons are basted in place, stitch along edges of each ribbon. Always work along the ribbon in the same direction on both sides so that it does not pucker if the stitching drags it.

6 Finish by pulling loose threads to the wrong side, then sew them in by hand. This neatens up unsightly ends and prevents stitching from coming undone during washing. Press with a cool iron.

Easy Bordered Tablecloth

Dress your table in style with a customized bordered tablecloth.

BEFORE YOU BEGIN

Personalize a tablecloth by designing it to highlight the shape of your dining table with stylish and professional-looking borders.

Making the Pattern

• Draw a rectangle the same size as your tabletop. Label AB.
• Add 10 inches to each side of rectangle AB to form larger rectangle CD.
• Draw diagonal lines from corners of AB to corners of CD.
• Draw border strips within rectangles AB and CD. Outer border: 3 inches wide, positioned 2 inches from raw edge. Inner border: 1 inch wide, positioned 1½ inches from finished table edge (the seam that joins piece 1 to pieces 4 and 7).
• Label pattern pieces as indicated. Mark top and bottom edges of each piece. Cut pieces 4 through 9 apart. Cut piece 1 (rectangle AB). Trace, then cut, pieces 2 and 3; do not cut them out of middle of piece 1. Add ½-inch seam allowance to all edges of all pieces.

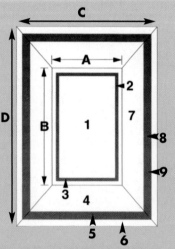

Cutting Layout

Cut the following pieces, adding seam allowances to all edges. Cut along grain of the fabric, keeping tops of all pieces running in the same direction. For pieces 4-9, make the second piece a mirror image of the first.

From tablecloth fabric: One inner tablecloth—cut one from piece 1. Two each of upper drop—pieces 4 and 7. Two each of lower drop—pieces 6 and 9.

From border fabric: Two each of inner border strips—pieces 2 and 3. Two each of outer border strips—pieces 5 and 8.

Sewing the Tablecloth

1 With right sides together, sew long edges of pieces 4 and 5. Then stitch piece 5 to 6 to complete shorter panel of outer drop. Press seam allowances open.

2 As in Step 1, sew pieces 7-8-9 to form longer panels of outer drop. With right sides together, sew panels 4-5-6 to panels 7-8-9 to make rectangle. Leave ½ inch open at both ends of seams.

3 With right sides together, join short edges of border pieces 2 and 3 at 45-degree angle. Leave ½ inch open at inside edge of seam. Join remaining inner border strips to form rectangle; press seams open.

4 Press under ½ inch along long unfinished edges of inner border. Measure and pin border 2 inches from raw edge of center panel piece. Stitch close to folded edges, pivoting at corners; press seams open.

5 With right sides together, stitch drop panels to center panel, matching corners. Pivot, catching points of drop panel corners. Make sure extra fabric is not caught in stitching. Clip corners; press seams open.

6 Press under ¼ inch and then ¼ inch again on outer edges of tablecloth. Stitch close to inner fold. Press entire tablecloth. Neaten wrong side by trimming seam allowances and any loose threads.

DECORATIVE WIRED-FABRIC RIBBON

Wired-fabric ribbon is easy to make and complements any decor.

YOU WILL NEED

❏ FABRIC

❏ SHEARS

❏ IRON

❏ 5MM-GAUGE WIRE & WIRE CUTTER

❏ SEWING MACHINE

❏ THREAD

❏ YARDSTICK

BEFORE YOU BEGIN

Create exactly the ribbon you want, with just the right width, fabric and color—and save a huge amount of money in the bargain.

Determining Ribbon Measurements

• Use a string to determine length of fabric strip. Wrap string around basket and tie a big bow in same fashion as you will fabric ribbon; add 1 inch for hems.
• Determine desired finished width of ribbon. Ours was 2 inches wide for napkin rings, 3 inches wide for basket bow and 4 inches wide for curtain tiebacks.

Napkin Rings

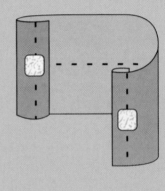

For napkin rings without a bow, cut, stitch and hem ribbon as instructed. Apply hook and loop fastener tape to ends of wired ribbon, hook piece on right side of fabric and loop piece on wrong side. Alternatively, eliminate fasteners by stitching ends to create a continuous loop.

Tiebacks

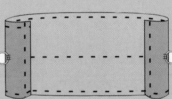

For tiebacks, cut, stitch and hem wired ribbon as instructed. On each short end, stitch a small plastic ring to turned-under edge of tieback. Hook rings on cup hooks attached to window molding or wall. For floor-length curtains, position tiebacks about two-thirds of the way from the floor. When curtains are closed, tiebacks can be stored on a hook behind curtain.

SEWING WIRED-FABRIC RIBBON

DOLLAR SENSE

Purchase less fabric by cutting the strips crosswise rather than lengthwise on the fabric. Stitch the short ends of several strips together to equal the full cutting length of the strip.

QUICK FIX

Instead of sewing hems, apply a liquid sealant to prevent fraying. By using this clean-finishing method, the ribbon tails can be angle cut or notched for added interest.

1 Cut a determined length of fabric equal to 2 times finished width plus ½ inch. With right sides together, fold fabric in half lengthwise. Making a ¼-inch seam allowance, stitch long sides together to create a tube.

2 Turn back a few inches of fabric to right side, creating a cuff. Insert yardstick into cuff. Gently push yardstick and pull cuff to turn tube right side out. Press flat with seam centered between folds.

3 Cut two wires, each 3 inches longer than fabric length. Attach one end of each wire to yardstick with tape. Insert into tube, feeding wire through to other end. Remove tape and slide yardstick out of tube.

4 Position one piece of wire at each long side of fabric tube. Using zipper foot, stitch as close as possible to each edge of fabric, enclosing wire between stitches and long edges of fabric.

5 Cut wire ends even with raw ends of fabric. To finish and prevent fabric ends from raveling, turn under fabric and wire; press ½ inch to inside. Stitch hems in place, taking care to avoid wires.

6 Wrap ribbon around a basket and tie a bow. Work loops and tails of bow to desired shape. Also use wired fabric ribbon to create napkin rings, curtain tiebacks or any other decorative accents.

NATURALLY EMBELLISHED TABLE LINENS

Customize table linens using paint and materials from nature.

YOU WILL NEED

❑ LEAVES
❑ TABLECLOTH & NAPKINS
❑ FABRIC PAINT
❑ FOAM ROLLERS
❑ PLASTIC KITCHEN
   CUTTING BOARD
❑ TAILOR'S CHALK
❑ SCRAP PAPER
❑ TYPING PAPER
❑ IRON & PRESS CLOTH

BEFORE YOU BEGIN

Design a foliage motif using the prettiest leaves you can find to create a charming tablecloth and napkin ensemble.

Choosing the Right Materials

• Flat, woven fabrics in cotton, linen, or cotton/poly blends are the best surfaces for printing. Decorating textured and novelty fabrics can produce unusual results. Sometimes the design becomes slightly obscured and more abstract.

• Whether using raw fabric or a purchased tablecloth and napkins, prewash each piece to remove any sizing left from the manufacturing process. Press the fabric well to remove wrinkles and to obtain a flat printing surface. Experiment on a scrap of fabric first.

• Finish the raw edges of the fabric with an overlock stitch, or turn the raw edges under ¼ inch twice, and stitch for a nice, narrow hem.

• Use tailor's chalk to mark the placement of the leaf design on the pressed fabric.

• Use water-based fabric paints in any color. Have basic black and white on hand to mix with the standard, prepared colors to achieve variations in color and tone.

• Use airtight containers to mix paints and to store leftover paints for future use.

Finding Leaves

• Find leaves that have interesting silhouettes as well as pronounced and detailed veins such as tulip tree, hedge, maple, black oak, willow and linden (below).

• Use green leaves that are fresh and pliable and not too fragile. Discard them when they curl or become dry and brittle.

• Sturdier flowers like daisies, chrysanthemums, and sunflowers create interesting imprints and continue the botanical theme.

• Materials can be preserved for several days by placing them flat in an airtight plastic bag and storing them in the refrigerator or in another cool place.

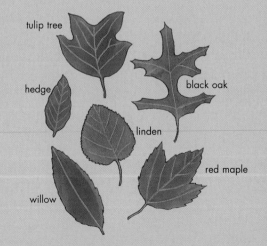

tulip tree

hedge

black oak

linden

willow

red maple

PRINTING ON FABRIC WITH LEAVES

1 Working with one color at a time, pour a small amount of paint onto a plastic kitchen cutting board or a piece of glass. Roll a foam roller through the paint so that the entire surface is covered with paint.

2 Place a leaf, face down, on a scrap of paper. Roll an even amount of paint over the entire leaf. Applying the paint to the underside of the leaf where the veins are more pronounced leaves a stronger image.

3 Using the tailor's chalk marks on the fabric as placement guides (Before you Begin), position the leaf, paint side down, on the right side of the fabric. Once the leaf has touched the fabric, do not move it.

4 Place a sheet of thin paper, such as typing paper, over the leaf. Using a clean roller, press over the leaf, rolling back and forth a few times. Make sure the paper does not move during the rolling process.

5 Gently pull back the paper and lift the leaf from the fabric. Repeat the printing process (Steps 1–5), varying leaves. To protect the designs when laundering, press the leaf prints using a warm iron and press cloth.

CREATE
STYLE

Rooms don't just create their own style. You give it to them. But that requires a theme and some concepts. Then a final plan. And of course the projects for carrying out the vision. Here's how to create that style, fine-tuned precisely to you and your tastes. Chapters include:

- *Making Beautiful Window Seats*
- *Highlighting the Effects of Line*
- *Decorating with Distinct Style*
- *Decorating with Sheets*

MAKING BEAUTIFUL WINDOW SEATS

Transform a window recess into an attractive and functional alcove.

MAKING IT WORK

A cozy, pillow-filled window seat is perfect for whiling away lazy daytime hours.

A Place to Daydream

• Build a platform into a window recess. Then top it with a thick **seat cushion** (page 102) to create a cozy nook.

• Decorative molding on the front of the seat gives the whole area a more sophisticated look.

• Make a thick, sturdy **cushion** (page 102) for the platform. Use good quality foam blocks; they are easy to cut and fit into any shaped area.

• Make several throw **pillows** (pages 104, 106) in a variety of fabrics to introduce pat-

tern, color and a feeling of warmth to the window seat and create a perfect place for idle daydreaming.

• Tailored **Roman shades** (page 108) suit the large expanse of windows. They can be closed quickly for privacy at night.

• White molding around the window recess clearly sets the window seat apart from the rest of the room.

VARIATIONS ON A THEME

Babes in Toyland

• Build **wood shelving** (page 110) around a single window for storage and display. Build shelves right onto the wall or purchase single shelf units and join them to frame the window. Nail or screw free-standing units to the wall to prevent a child from pulling them over.

• Use a brightly colored box as a dual-purpose toy box and window seat. As the child gets older, replace the toy box with cabinets painted to match the surrounding shelves. Put pillows on top to make a comfy seat.

Hidden Possibilities

• An attractive radiator cover with inset screens is more elegant than a visible radiator. They can be purchased in many different styles and sizes.

• Add a cushion and matching throw pillows to the top of the radiator cover, and the room gains a charming window nook.

• Three-quarter-length curtains frame and highlight the window area. Position the tiebacks at cushion level to add an accent, and pull the curtains around the window seat.

READY FOR BED

When nighttime comes, just remove the throw pillows and pull out bed linens you've stashed nearby.
• Coordinate the cushion cover and sheets for a smartly designed sleeping area.
• Keep a set of sheets, a spare pillow and a blanket stored nearby for a quick transformation at bedtime.
• Convert the window seat platform into a hinged lid. The space underneath can be used for easily accessible storage.

CASUAL WINDOW SEAT CUSHION

A comfortable cushion softens the sharp angles of a window seat.

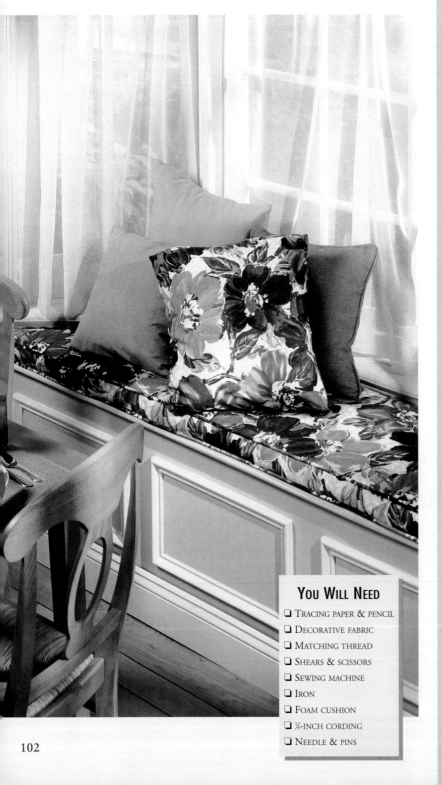

BEFORE YOU BEGIN

Sewing a window seat cushion is just as simple as sewing a chair cushion.

Pattern and Cutting Pointers

To make a pattern, lay tracing paper on top of the window seat and trace its outline. Lift paper, add ½-inch seam allowances on all sides; then cut out the pattern. Lay the pattern on top of the seat to check accuracy.

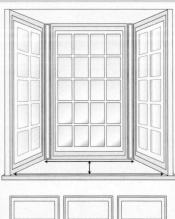

To determine the fabric needed, measure the seat depth times 2, then add three yards for the boxing strips and welting. To cut, open the fabric and lay it right side up on a flat surface. Follow the layout (right) for placing cushion pattern pieces. This will allow the fabric pattern to run in the same direction for both top and bottom pieces.

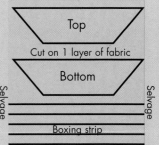

For the boxing strips, refer to the diagram and cut out several 4-inch-wide strips the width of the fabric. Sew the strips together to make the sides of the seat cushion.

Use remaining fabric to make the bias strips for welting.

Cushion and Cording Prep

For the cushion, cut a 3-inch-thick piece of foam the same size as the window seat. (Use an electric knife to cut foam.) For best results, choose a firm foam made especially for seat cushions; some will be prewrapped with cotton batting.

To make the welting, measure the circumference of the cushion, add 6 inches; multiply by 2. Cut 1½-inch bias strips from the fabric; piece together to make one long strip. Wrong sides facing, fold strip over cording; stitch close to cord using zipper foot.

MAKING A WINDOW SEAT CUSHION

1 Pin pattern for cushion top and bottom; cut out both. Measure and cut boxing strips, starting close to cut edge of fabric piece. From remaining fabric, cut bias strips and make welting (Before you Begin).

2 With raw edges aligned, pin and baste welting to the right side of the cushion top. Repeat for the cushion bottom. Clip the welting seam allowances so that they ease around the corners.

3 To join the raw edges of the welting, trim away ½ inch to 1 inch of the inside cording on one end. Fold the raw edge of the fabric under, then overlap the welting ends. Pin and baste in place.

4 With right sides facing and raw edges aligned, stitch short sides of the boxing strips together. Make one long strip to fit around all four cushion sides, plus a 1-inch seam allowance.

5 With right sides together and raw edges aligned, stitch the two remaining boxing strip ends together with a 1-inch seam. Pin the boxing strip, right sides facing, around top of the cushion. To ensure catching the welting in the seam when stitching, feed the fabric into the sewing machine with the cushion top fabric up and stitch just outside of the welting basting line.

6 Using a zipper foot, stitch the cushion top to the boxing strip. Make sure to leave one long side open for turning. Next, pin and stitch the cushion bottom to the boxing strip.

7 Clip the corners through all fabric layers so that the sides, top, bottom and welting fit together smoothly. Turn the cover right side out and insert the foam through the opening in the seat cushion; adjust so the welting lies directly around the top and bottom edges of the sides. The foam should fit snugly into the cushion corners. Pin the opening closed; slipstitch with a needle and matching thread.

LACE-STENCILED PILLOWS

Make unique pillows with fabric created by stenciling through a lace panel.

YOU WILL NEED

- ❏ FABRIC
- ❏ PILLOW FORM
- ❏ PIPING OR CORDING
- ❏ LACE PANEL
- ❏ WOOD FOR FRAME
- ❏ WOOD GLUE & NAILS
- ❏ STAPLE GUN & HAMMER
- ❏ TEXTILE PAINT
- ❏ PAINT STABILIZER
- ❏ SPRAY GUN
- ❏ TISSUE OR LIGHT-
   WEIGHT FABRIC
- ❏ SEWING MACHINE
- ❏ NEEDLE & THREAD
- ❏ IRON

BEFORE YOU BEGIN

Stenciling with lace is an easy way to design fabrics that coordinate perfectly with a desired color scheme.

Lace and Fabric Requirements

When purchasing lace for stenciling purposes, select a lace that has at least two repeats in the width of the fabric. Purchase enough yardage for two lengthwise repeats of the design to cover the pillow top, plus 6 to 8 inches for attaching the fabric to the frame.

Select a lace with an all-over motif when stenciling an all-over design.

Purchase ½ yard of fabric for each 16-inch pillow cover. Fabrics with a smooth texture, such as tightly woven, medium-weight cotton like broadcloth or muslin, work best to create a clear print of the lace design.

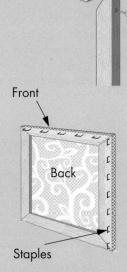

Making the Frame and Stencil

Make a frame for the lace stencil from four equal-sized pieces of flat, wood molding 8 inches shorter than the width of the lace. Miter each piece of molding at both ends.

Join the wood at the corners with wood glue or nails. If opting for nails, the nails should go through the outer edge of one panel into the mitered edge of the adjoining panel (top right).

Center the frame on the lace and fold the lace edges over the frame. Staple the lace edges to the back of the frame (bottom right). The lace should be taut, but not over-stretched.

Front

Back

Staples

STENCILING WITH LACE

TAKE NOTE

Always wear a mask when using spray paints. Disposable masks are available at craft supply or hardware stores.

QUICK FIX

If stenciling a pillowcase or other tubular item, remember to put a protective layer inside so the paint doesn't seep through to the back.

1 Prior to stenciling, tape several layers of clean paper over work surface to protect it. Tape prewashed, premeasured fabric to padded work surface and outline border on fabric with tape, if necessary.

2 Position lace-covered frame on top of fabric. Mix textile paint with paint stabilizer until it is the right consistency (check manufacturer's instructions). Fill spray gun; spray on fabric. Paint will transfer through lace.

3 After completing painting process, remove stretched-lace frame. Place tissue or lightweight fabric on top of stenciled design; set design onto fabric using an iron at a moderate heat setting.

4 From coordinating fabric, cut bias strips wide enough to wrap around cord plus two seam allowances. Stitch lengths of bias together making one continuous strip. Wrap cord; stitch fabric close to cording, using zipper foot.

5 Stitch covered cord to stenciled fabric using edge as guide. At corners, reduce stitch length and slightly curve corners, slowly guiding, but not stretching, piping taut. Join piping ends for finished look.

6 With right sides together, stitch corded, stenciled fabric to backing fabric. Be sure to leave opening for turning and stuffing pillow. Clip corners; turn pillow right side out. Stuff with pillow form or other stuffing of choice. Slipstitch opening closed, or close with hook-and-loop fastener tape on seam allowances, to make removal of pillow from pillowcase easier.

CREATIVELY EDGED THROW PILLOWS

Add style and zip to plain throw pillows with overlapping triangle trim.

YOU WILL NEED

- ❏ FAUX SUEDE
- ❏ ROTARY CUTTER OR SHEARS
- ❏ FUSIBLE INTERFACING
- ❏ SEWING MACHINE
- ❏ THREAD. NEEDLE & PINS
- ❏ TAPE MEASURE
- ❏ IRON
- ❏ CLEAR GRID RULER

BEFORE YOU BEGIN

Faux suede, felt and polar fleece are great fabrics to use because they're washable, can be cut precisely and don't ravel.

Creating a Pattern

Determine the finished length of the pillow sides to find the measurement of the fabric triangles for the edging.

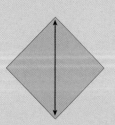

- Cut the fabric for pillow front and back to the finished sized plus ½ inch on all sides for seams.
- Divide the pillow side length by three. This measurement is the length of the diagonal of each fabric square (above). Add 1 inch to the diagonal length for overlapping the triangles.
- Using a ruler and a chalk marker, mark the diagonal measurement along two edges of the fabric. With a T square, draw right angles from the points to make six squares (left). Cut out the fabric squares with a rotary cutter.

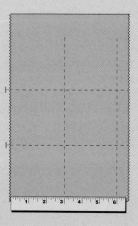

Painting Preparation

The best stay tape to use for stabilizing the triangles is a woven fusible interfacing. Using a clear, gridded ruler and a rotary cutter, cut 1-inch-wide strips. Cut the interfacing in the direction that is the most stable. This is usually the lengthwise grain line.

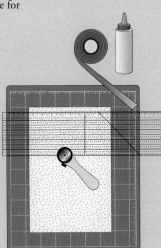

When fusible interfacing is not available, you can stabilize the triangle edge by using prepackaged seam tape. Adhere the seam tape to the fabric with fabric glue or by edgestitching.

Making the Pillow Trim

1 Place three fabric squares (Before you Begin) on an ironing surface, with right sides down. Evenly overlap the corners of the squares so the diagonal line formed is equal to the length of one pillow side.

2 Lay the 1-inch strips of fusible interfacing (Before you Begin), fusible side down, through the squares' centers, along the diagonal line. Press with a warm iron for 12 seconds. Trim the interfacing.

3 Using polyester thread and a regular stitch length, machine stitch along one edge of the interfacing through all the layers. Repeat the edgestitching along the opposite edge of the fusible strip.

HANDY HINTS

Faux suede is easy to handle, but requires a few reminders: Press with a medium hot iron; use a 80/12 universal needle and a good quality polyester thread.

DOLLAR SENSE

Purchase faux suede scraps by the bag. It is less expensive to buy them this way and the colors come mixed in a fun assortment.

4 Lay triangles, right side down, on a cutting mat. With a rotary cutter, cut down the center of the fusible interfacing. The ½-inch-wide strip becomes the side seam allowance. Repeat Steps 1–4 for the remaining three squares.

5 With right sides together, position a strip of attached triangles to one pillow edge. Stitch through all the layers over the previous edgestitching line. Repeat procedure for the remaining pillow side edges.

6 With right sides together, sew the sections to form the pillow, using the previous stitching line as a guide. Leave an opening along one side. Trim and clip corners. Turn and insert the pillow form; slipstitch closed.

NO-SEW ROMAN SHADE

This custom shade is surprisingly easy to make.

BEFORE YOU BEGIN

Fusible tape makes this a quick project to create. To hang, simply attach to a mounting board in the window.

Measuring for Fabric and Tape

Roman shades require a minimal amount of fabric.
• Measure the inside length and width of the window.
• Cut fabric so width is 2½ inches wider than the inside window width and 5½ inches longer than the inside window length.

• Purchase enough fusible ring tape to equal four times the length of the shade.
• Buy fusible hem tape to equal two times the length of shade plus two times width plus 4 inches.
• Purchase the tape with protective release paper.

Making a Mounting Board

A wood board fastened to the upper inside window frame (right) holds the shade hardware and hook-and-loop fastener tape that keeps the shade in place. Normally, the shade is attached to the board, then mounted in window.

Attach a drapery cleat to the wall for securing the cords.

Measure inside width of window and cut a ¾-inch-thick by 1½-inch-wide board to that measurement. Screw angle brackets to underside of board at edges (right).

Determine placement of ring tapes on shade. Attach screw eyes to mounting board, copying placement of ring tape. Secure mounting board to inner window frame.

Cords travel through rings up each row of tape on shade, through a matching screw eye on mounting board and across board to one side.

CREATING A ROMAN SHADE

HANDY HINTS

If a lot of light hits the window, line the shade with a light-colored, firmly woven cotton fabric.

If fusible ring tape is not available, fuse using fusible web between tape and fabrics.

1 For side hems, fold fabric 1¼ inches to wrong side; press. Open fold and pin fusible hem tape close to raw edge on wrong side. Remove protective paper after ironing in place. Close fold and iron to fuse hem.

2 For top hem, fold fabric ¾ inch to wrong side; press. Add hem tape and fuse as in Step 1. Pin loop side of fusible hook-and-loop fastener tape over hem, covering fused edge. Fuse in place, removing pins.

3 At bottom of shade, fold ¾ inch to wrong side and fuse hem tape. Fold again, 4 inches from edge, and fuse hem in place. Fuse a 2-inch-long strip of hem tape at lower side edges, but leave an opening to insert weight rod.

TAKE NOTE

Use liquid seam protector to keep ends of ring tape and nylon cord from fraying with use. Also apply to cut edges of fabrics that tend to ravel.

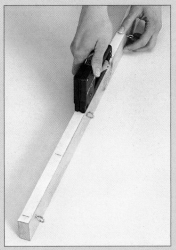

4 Pin ring tape in place: one row over each side edge and two rows set at equal distances in center of shade. Rings must be at same height in each row. Remove pins as you fuse ring tape in place.

5 Attach screw eyes to underside of mounting board, placing them at the same position as ring tapes. Using a staple gun, secure hook side of hook-and-loop fastener tape to front side of mounting board.

6 Mount shade on board, matching hook-and-loop tapes. Tie nylon cords to bottom ring of each tape. Thread cord through rings and screws and across top. Insert weight rod in opening of hem.

CUSTOMIZED WOODEN SHELVES

Add style and storage with some simple, decorative shelves.

YOU WILL NEED

- ❏ 1x10 & 1x12
  PIECES OF PINE LUMBER
- ❏ 1⅜-INCH-DIAMETER
  FLUTED CURTAIN ROD
- ❏ CLOSET ROD BRACKETS
- ❏ WOOD STAIN
- ❏ DRILL & DRILL BIT
- ❏ SCREWS & WOOD GLUE
- ❏ SANDPAPER
- ❏ PUTTY & PUTTY KNIFE
- ❏ PENCIL & RULER
- ❏ MOUNTING HARDWARE

BEFORE YOU BEGIN

Alter the elements and measurements so the shelf will fit on your wall or around your window. Stain or paint the shelf unit as desired.

Measuring and Cutting Wood

For this shelf unit, you will need to cut two pieces from 1x10 lumber 31 inches long for the sides, and two 20½-inch-long pieces for the shelves. For the top, you will need to cut a 24-inch-long piece from a 1x12 board.

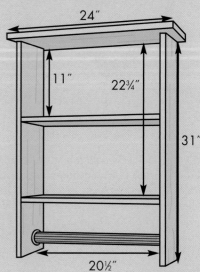

For the rod, purchase a 1⅜-inch-diameter fluted curtain rod or dowel that is 20½ inches long minus twice the depth of a rod bracket.

Tips for Assembling the Shelf

Before screwing pieces of the shelf together, always drill a pilot hole narrower than the screw. This keeps the wood from splitting and makes inserting the screws easier and faster.

Mark the position of the screw. Then begin pilot holes by drilling a hole ⅛ inch into the wood. This allows the screw to be countersunk into the wood.

Pine is a good choice to use for shelves, but often has natural curves in the wood. To disguise the curves, position so the wood curves upward for the shelves and toward the inside for the sides of the shelves.

Closet rod brackets can be purchased from hardware stores and are available in both wood and metal. Metal brackets have either brass or silver finishes.

The placement line for the screws should fall exactly between the lines marking the top and bottom of each shelf. Otherwise, the tip of the screws could surface above or below the shelf instead of drilling directly into the center.

MAKING A SHELF UNIT

1 Sand the wood smooth. Mark the shelf placement at 11 inches and 22¾ inches on the sides. Draw additional lines ¾ inch underneath the first two. Mark three evenly spaced screw placements between the shelf lines.

2 Drill three pilot holes for each shelf. Measure and mark placement for closet rod brackets on the inside of each side, 3 inches from bottom of shelf and 3 inches in from front edge. Drill pilot holes; fasten with screws.

3 Apply wood glue to side of top shelf. Join shelf to one side, then screw in place. Repeat for lower shelf and rod; glue and screw remaining side in place. Center and screw top to shelf with back flush to sides.

DOLLAR SENSE

Many hardware stores keep bins full of short leftover pieces of wood ideal for shelves. These are inexpensive.

TAKE NOTE

When hanging the shelf, be sure to mount the hardware into a wall stud. If you can't find a stud underneath the sheetrock where you wish to hang the shelf, use a toggle screw to hang the shelf.

4 Using a putty knife, fill screw holes on all sides of shelf with wood filler. When dry, sand filler and all sides of shelf smooth with a fine grade sandpaper. Wipe away dust with a damp cloth.

5 Cover a flat surface with newspaper, then position shelf on top. With sponge brush, paint a light coat of stain on the shelf. Let dry, then add a second coat if desired, sanding and wiping clean between each coat.

6 When the stain is completely dry, mark 6 inches from the top on the back edges of the shelf unit. Following manufacturer's instructions, attach flush mount shelf hardware to each side. Drill pilot holes for hardware and screw in place. Hang shelf unit on wall.

HIGHLIGHTING THE EFFECTS OF LINE

Manipulating the line of furnishings and accessories creates a unique style in any room.

MAKING IT WORK

Once you've determined the effect you want to achieve, let the lines of the furnishings help you carry out your decorating plan.

Curvy Comfort

• Curves create a welcoming mood. Choose furniture and accessories that feature dominant curves, but add a few decorative elements with straight lines for contrast.

• When curves dominate a room, use minimal accessories that don't compete with the larger elements, so that the effect of the curves is not lost.

• Arching the valance at the top of the window prevents a straight line from breaking up the curvy feel of the room.

• Repetition of particular lines helps form a rhythm within the room. A circular gold-framed mirror, oval mahogany coffee table and circular area rug

create the curves that are echoed through the room.

• Unity in a decor is strongest when its direction comes not only from the walls and furniture, but also from the small details elsewhere in the room.

• The sensuous curve of this sofa's arms leads the eye to the many curves in the adjacent fabrics and wallpaper. **Adding trim to upholstered furniture** (page 114) can enhance the lines of particular furniture pieces.

• The patterned damask, floral fabrics and sophisticated wallpaper pattern feature the same fluid lines and shapes.

VARIATIONS ON A THEME

Horizontal

• For the clean, straight lines of contemporary decor, most accessories and furniture in this room were chosen for their linear properties.

• Light, thinner lines appear farther away than dark or thicker lines. The soft lines of the wainscoting push the walls out, making the room seem larger.

• A chair rail and horizontal wainscoting wrap **lower walls** (page 118), continuing the room's illusion of width. Completing the effect, **linear photo displays** (page 116) rest on shelves made of molding.

Diagonal

• In a room with little architectural detail, emphasize the interesting angles of the vaulted ceiling by adding a colorful border design.

• Bright blue molding and a **wall border** (pages 120, 122) highlight the roofline. Plan lines carefully: Narrow lines can fade back, while wider stripes may become overpowering.

• Angling the garden bench across the room's corner prevents too vertical a look and makes the setting more cozy and inviting.

Vertical

• Visually heighten a room by incorporating vertical elements. Dramatic wallpaper stripes are the most obvious choice for leading the eye upward. Stack frames instead of lining them horizontally.

• Cleverly build on this vertical theme by using similar lines in accessories. Here, the gathers of the **pleated blinds** (page 124) and the **circular tablecloth** (page 126) folds pull the eye upward.

• Choose furniture that reinforces the vertical theme, such as a four-poster bed.

ADDED TRIM FOR UPHOLSTERED FURNITURE

Easy-to-apply trims define lines and add flair to furniture.

BEFORE YOU BEGIN

Choose from a wealth of fabric embellishments to create a finished look that can range from elegant to sleek to downright comfy.

Types of Trims

Fabric stores and craft shops market a vast selection of trims.

Cording varies from graceful twists ideal for accenting curves to heavy rope for boxy outlines.

Heavy, rope-like bullion fringe, traditionally shot through with metallic threads, gives an opulent finish. Use it on substantial furniture covered with damask, brocade and the like.

Delicate fringes seem at home paired with boudoir chairs and dining room seats upholstered with satin, watered silk or velvet.

Ball fringe, especially in primary colors, brings back memories of '50s curtains and can add a fun retro touch to an informal room.

Gimp, or flat braid, lends a neat, unfussy finish, perfect for conservatively tailored slipcovers.

Eyelet lace looks dainty and romantic on gingham and florals; choose the bound-edge variety for easier application.

Novelty trims, with geometric, cute or humorous motifs, work well on informal kitchen chairs and children's furniture.

Trim Tricks

• Always cut a bit more trim than you think you really need to allow for curves, tucks and thread tension as you stitch.
• To decorate any upholstered furniture, use trim to cover seam lines all around.

Apply with hot glue, needle and thread, upholstery tacks, or a combination.
• Dab liquid seam protector onto cut ends of trims and let dry before pinning in place.

Trimming an Ottoman

1 Pin trim in place around the circumference of the ottoman, with the trim's flat edge toward the bottom. Unravel ends slightly and weave together for a smooth finish; stitch together securely.

2 Using a long upholstery needle and matching upholstery thread, carefully stitch the flat woven edge of the trim to the ottoman fabric. Keep stitch lengths even; don't pull too hard on the thread.

3 Tape the ends of the bullion fringe to prevent raveling. Pin in place, covering the flat edge of the braided trim and leaving a little extra to overlap at the end. Stitch the fringe to the braided trim's flat edge.

HANDY HINTS

Choose trim with finished edges to apply to completed upholstery. Save piping and other raw-edged trims for cushions and slipcovers pieced together from scratch.

Upholstery thread and buttonhole twist, designed for heavy-duty use, work well with thick layers of fabric and trim. Achieve a similar effect by running regular thread across a block of beeswax.

Pushing an upholstery needle through layers of heavy fabric and thick trim can prove tough on soft hands. Use a thimble on your middle finger or thumb for protection and power.

4 When you come to the end of the bullion fringe, fold under the loose end by about ½ inch (enough to attach securely). Place the folded edge over the raw edge at the beginning of the fringe, overlapping slightly, and stitch in place through all the layers.

DOLLAR SENSE

Save leftover bits and pieces of trim for decorating pillows to match.

LINEAR PHOTO DISPLAYS

Arrange your favorite photographs in a novel horizontal display.

YOU WILL NEED

- ❏ BRASS ROD
- ❏ FINIALS
- ❏ MOUNTING HARDWARE
- ❏ S HOOKS
- ❏ GOLD ROPE OR BRAID
- ❏ FRAMED PICTURES
- ❏ GLUE GUN & GLUE STICKS

BEFORE YOU BEGIN

Look for unique ways to hang your pictures, so that the display becomes a real conversation piece in the room.

Hanging Variations

 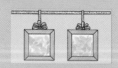

A sturdy branch gathered from the garden makes a unique rod for hanging pictures to enhance a rustic decor.

To complete the country feeling, choose pictures with outdoor themes and frame them in natural wood. Add the perfect finishing touch by using rough string or rope to hang the pictures from the branch.

Decorate a wooden rod to enhance a pair of floral prints. Pick out colors from the pictures or frames and use them to paint a floral design along the length of the rod.

Alternatively, wrap ribbon along the length of the rod and then use the same ribbon to hang the pictures. For dramatic effect, tie the ribbon in a fancy bow.

Copper tubing, available at any plumbing supply store, makes an inexpensive, modern picture rod. Add end caps to give a more finished look and suspend it from beaded chains.

Almost any ring can be used to hang the pictures, from shower curtain rings to metal bracelets.

Suspend oars in opposite directions from plain, wrought iron hooks. Leave the oar locks on for interest.

Hang the pictures at different heights using nautical rope tied in a variety of different sailor's knots.

HANGING THE PICTURES

1 Hang pictures at eye level. Taking length of S hooks and cord into account, determine position of rod and mark it on wall in pencil. Follow manufacturer's instructions to mount wall brackets.

2 Suspend rod from wall-mounted brackets. Add decorative finials at each end. Measure area to be covered with pictures. Work out a good arrangement on floor to determine hanging cord lengths.

3 Use hot glue to attach appropriate lengths of gold rope to back of each picture to make hanging cords. If pictures are heavy, hammer small tacks or nails into glued area for additional security.

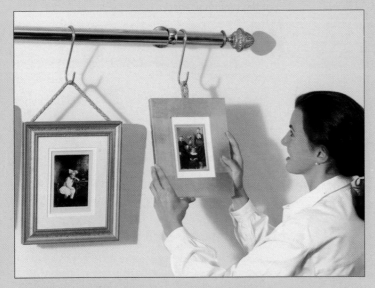

4 Hang S hooks from rod. Once glue has dried on back of frames, suspend pictures from hooks in previously determined formation. Different-length cords and different-size frames will add dimension and visual interest to display.

HANDY HINTS

If the pictures are to hang opposite a sunny window or bright light fixture, consider mounting them behind non-reflective glass.

Same-size frames with related subject matter look best when hung in a symmetrical or straight manner.

TAKE NOTE

Displays of two or more same-size pictures must be hung at eye level.

For pictures hung above a sofa, make sure that the lowest frame is well above head height, and that the picture group does not extend beyond the sofa width.

QUICK FIX

Hanging cords need not be expensive to be effective. Consider ribbon, shoestrings, braid, webbing, raffia or rope to help create a unique display.

LOWER WALL COVERING OPTIONS

Embellish lower walls with these clever decorating techniques.

BEFORE YOU BEGIN

Wallpaper and paint aren't the only options for covering walls. With a bit of imagination, you can turn a plain surface into a unique backdrop.

Creative Options

• Painting the wall with chalkboard paint is a clever way to decorate a room. Paint several coats so the finish will be thick enough to withstand repeated use and cleanings. Add a chair rail wide enough to hold pieces of chalk.

• Inexpensive reed fencing purchased from building supply stores or garden centers can be cut to size and stapled along the lower part of a wall. If desired, paint the reed to match your decor.

• Apply a favorite fabric around a wall as if it were wallpaper.

• Flat sheets of tin or copper can be pieced to cover a wall.

• In a child's room or a home office, cover a lower wall with dry erase board (below left). This offers a permanent drawing surface for a youngster's artwork or a busy worker's lists, notes or formulas. The wall is easily and quickly cleaned for future use.

• Create a message center or photo gallery by applying corkboard tiles around the wall (below right). Corkboard can also be purchased in rolls, or sheets, at hardware and home supply stores. Paint the corkboard a vibrant color or leave it natural.

Finishing Walls

If your wall does not already have a chair rail, add your own to hide the edges of your lower wall treatment.

• Chair molding is available in a variety of sizes and styles. Choose one that complements your wall.

• Chair moldings can be purchased from building supply stores. Measure the walls; then have molding cut to size.

• For best results, paint the molding before attaching it to the wall. Cover nail holes with touch-up paint.

COVERING THE WALL

1 Using a utility knife, cut the bamboo rod from the matchstick blinds. Remove the hardware and several of the matchsticks, then tie the strings together to keep from raveling.

2 Using a wallpaper brush, apply a generous amount of wallpaper paste to the wall. Cover an area only as large as the first blind, and be sure to wipe drips off the floor.

3 Beginning at one corner or at the end of the wall, carefully unroll the blind across the lower section of the wall, pressing the matchsticks into the wallpaper paste as you work. Work as quickly as possible, and apply more wallpaper paste if needed to secure the blind to the wall.

4 Once the blind has been secured to the wall, wipe away excess wallpaper paste with a damp sponge. Continue adding paste and matchstick blinds until the wall is covered.

SPONGE-PRINTED WALL BORDER

Sponge on shapes and splashes of color to add style to a plain wall.

BEFORE YOU BEGIN

This project is ready to start with only a few preparatory steps.

Preparing to Paint

• Measure the area where the sponge printing will go. Make sure the planned designs will fit in that space. Change the pattern if necessary to fit the available space.

• Draw the shapes onto sponges with a pen. Use scissors to cut out all sponge shapes prior to printing.

• Mix paint colors. Add white paint for a softer, more muted look. Pour some paint onto a tray large enough to hold the sponge shapes.

If sponge shape is too small to handle or is oddly shaped, glue it to an acrylic plastic or glass backing. Glue knob onto other side for easy handling.

Creating the Pattern

Draw the design on paper to determine shapes needed (right).

Keep number of forms to a minimum—more interest is easily added by using extra colors.

Add a shape that links the patterns together as the design progresses across the wall.

PRINTING SHAPES ON THE WALL

1 Use pencil or chalk to mark wall with placement marks for repeats. For horizontal repeats, use a level and straightedge for guidelines. This will keep the design in line as you proceed.

2 Keep paint trays and all sponges handy to print entire design. Dip sponge into paint and blot, if necessary. With a little paint on the sponge, press wall lightly to achieve a dappled look.

3 Latex paint is fast-drying, so quickly blot excess paint with a soft, clean sponge. Press sponge straight down on top of paint, and then lift straight up. Rinse sponge often for blotting other colors as you progress.

4 Add additional colors and shapes to complete the pattern. Work along horizontal guidelines to complete overall design. Stand back from your work and check that there are no blank areas that should be filled in. Add more shapes to any empty areas.

STAMPED WALL BORDER

Create unique stamps for painted wall treatments that match your room's style.

YOU WILL NEED

- ❏ 9- BY 12-INCH FOAM RUBBER, ⅛ INCH THICK
- ❏ CRAFT KNIFE
- ❏ GEL MEDIUM
- ❏ ACRYLIC PAINTS
- ❏ PAPER TOWELS
- ❏ SCRAP PAPER
- ❏ FINE-POINT PAINTBRUSH
- ❏ SMALL, FLAT PAINTBRUSH
- ❏ PLASTIC PLATE
- ❏ COTTON SWAB

BEFORE YOU BEGIN

Design planning and paint preparation are just as important as transferring the pattern to the wall. Follow these tips for certain success.

Stamping Success

• When choosing a stencil, pick a motif that suits the room. In addition, opt for a relatively simple motif that is easy to cut around with a craft knife.

• Use the stencil as a reference to plan a design on the wall. Then, draw light pencil guidelines (dotted line, below) according to the desired stamping design. This will ensure that the design remains on a straight line as it is stamped.

• To prevent smearing, never slide the stamp on the wall. Gently press the stamp onto the wall and tap with fingers to ensure an imprint. Carefully lift the stamp straight off the wall.

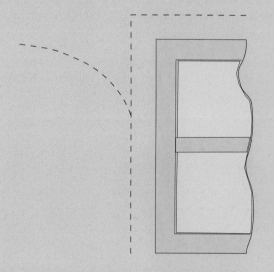

Paint Preparation

• Squeeze paint onto a plastic plate, then add a dab of gel medium and mix. Gel medium is available from craft and artist supply stores. It will keep the paint from drying out quickly and will give the stamped designs a translucent look.

• For a mottled effect, partially brush the stamp with one color, then add other colors as desired.

• The stamp will be held by a handle (see Step 1), so do not paint that part.

• If the design is not complete or is not dark enough after stamping, reapply paint to the stamp and restamp.

• Use a cotton swab to keep the scored lines free from paint build-up. This will allow the details to show up clearly.

STAMPING WALLS

TAKE NOTE

Stamping on a piece of scrap paper before stamping onto the wall will prevent smudges and paint build-up.

Always stamp on a clean, smooth surface.

OOPS

Keep a damp sponge and cotton swabs handy to remove mistakes.

1 Using a craft knife, cut the stamps from the foam rubber. Lightly score the inside lines for detail, being careful to cut only three-quarters of the way through the foam rubber. Remember to include a handle.

2 Paint the design on paper first. Use a flat paintbrush to paint the lines, then brush the stamps with paint and stamp the pattern on the paper. Use this paper as a placement diagram for painting the walls.

3 Lightly draw the design in pencil on the wall, making sure all the elements are well-balanced. Using the flat paintbrush, begin painting over the lines for the plant stems. Let dry completely.

4 Brush the scored side of the stamp with paint, then gently blot any excess paint with a paper towel. Holding the stamp by the handle, press it flat against the wall; then lift. Brush the stamp with paint as needed, remembering to avoid the handle.

5 Continue stamping the design onto the wall, varying the colors and shapes as desired. To layer the paint, stamp the background color of the design, let it dry, then stamp over the design with a different color paint.

6 Once the stamped design is dry, use the fine-point paintbrush to paint random tendrils on the wall. To avoid smearing the wet paint with your hand, work from one side of the wall to the other. Allow to dry overnight.

PLEATED LONDON BLINDS

Give windows a tailored style with this simple, classic blind.

BEFORE YOU BEGIN

This London blind variation gets its tailored look from pleats positioned over the ring tape section of the fabric.

Preparing the Fabric and Cord

• To determine the amount of fabric required, measure the inside length and width of the window.
• Add 12 inches to the width for each inverted pleat and 18 inches to the length for fullness. Add ½-inch seam allowance on all sides. Add the length of the fabric's pattern repeat if it is prominent and will be centered on the blind.
• Cut blind fabric and lining fabric to the above dimensions. Right sides facing, stitch the sides and bottom of the lining and fabric together; clip corners. Turn right side out; press seams flat. Stitch top edge closed.
• Use the guide (below) to mark pleat lines (Step 1).
• Cut two pieces of cord: one twice the length of the blind plus the width, and the other twice the length of the blind only.

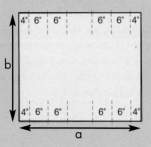

Installing the Blind

Secure the board inside the window recess using wood screws. Attach cleat inside the window frame, making sure it is hidden behind the blind. Wrap cords from blind around cleat to keep them tidy.

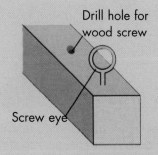

Drill hole for wood screw

Screw eye

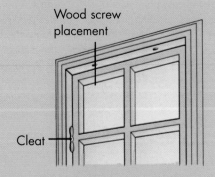

Wood screw placement

Cleat

MAKING A PLEATED LONDON BLIND

1 With lining side up, mark top and bottom edges of pleat folds with chalk. Make first mark 4 inches from the fabric side edge, the second mark 6 inches from the first and the third mark 6 inches from the second.

2 Center ring tape over second mark, positioning a ring at lower edge. Turn upper and lower tape edges under 1 inch. Machine stitch tape close to each side edge. Rings on each tape must be level.

3 Fold fabric along center of tape, right sides together, matching up first and third marks. Machine stitch along chalk line 3½ inches downward from upper edge and 3½ inches up from lower edge, securing ends.

4 Lay blind out flat. Position pleat so ring tape is directly above stitched pleats; press folds. Turn blind right side up and lay flat. Press pleat folds to lay flat and crisp. Repeat Steps 1–4 for remaining pleat.

5 Staple fabric to top edge of board. Attach eyescrews to bottom edge of board, making sure they align with ring tape and "eyes" face to sides. Insert one eyescrew at edge of board where cords will hang.

6 Tie nylon cord to bottom ring of each tape and run through rings to top. Thread through screw eyes, with longest cord threaded through all three. Trim cord ends to same length and tie together.

HANDY HINTS

For an added decorative touch, choose some pretty ribbon to match the blind fabric and stitch it to the front of the blind over the stitching that secures the tape.

For another finishing touch, add large, decorative buttons at the top of the pleat openings. Use buttons that are at least 2 inches in diameter.

TAKE NOTE

If the fabric has to be pieced together to fit a large window, try to ensure that the seams fall inside the pleats.

For extra flair on wide windows, add a ring tape and pleat in the center of the blind. To make a center pleat, mark the top and bottom edges at the center of the shade and again 6 inches from both sides of that mark for pleat folds and stitching.

EASY-TO-MAKE CIRCULAR TABLECLOTH

Whether its fabric is elegant or casual, a circular tablecloth adds style to any room.

BEFORE YOU BEGIN

Without very wide fabric, you must join widths together to make up the tablecloth. Making a paper pattern helps in cutting a perfect circle.

Measuring Up

For the diameter of a finished floor-length cloth, add the diameter of the tabletop to twice the height of the table. Add an extra 1½ inches to allow for a ¾-inch double-fold hem all around.

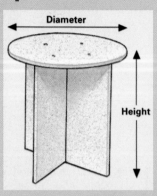

The total equals the outer dimensions of the square of fabric needed to make the circular cloth.

Joining Fabric Widths

If the fabric is narrower than the overall diameter of the planned tablecloth, join fabric widths before cutting out the circular cloth.
• Avoid seams that will fall across tabletops. They are unsightly and impractical.
• Use a full width of fabric for the central panel of the cloth. Join half widths of fabric down either side of the main panel as shown in the diagram (below).
• Join the selvages with a flat seam (right sides together and edges matching). Press seams open. If necessary, clip into the selvages to ensure that the seams lie flat.

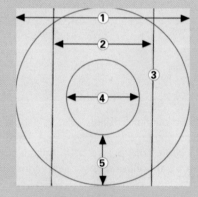

1. Overall measurement of fabric (including hems)
2. Full width of fabric
3. Position of seams
4. Diameter of tabletop
5. Height of table plus hem allowance

MAKING THE TABLECLOTH

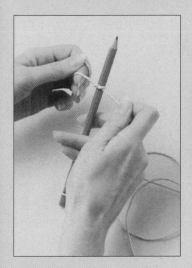

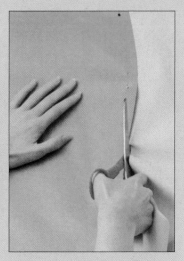

DOLLAR SENSE

Sheeting fabric is available in extra-wide widths, eliminating the need for seams on larger tablecloths. It is also an economical and easily washable type of fabric.

TAKE NOTE

Make sure shears are sharp enough to cut through several layers of fabric at the same time. Test them on scraps of fabric first so you won't ruin the tablecloth fabric.

1 Tie one end of a piece of string to a pencil. Measure from the pencil along the string a distance equal to half the cloth diameter (including hem) and mark. Tie a thumbtack to the string at this mark. Trim string.

2 Take a square sheet of paper slightly larger than the length of the string. Lay the paper on a work surface and push the thumbtack in at one corner. Pull string taut and draw a quarter circle. Cut out carefully.

3 Fold the fabric in half, and then in half again to make a smaller square. Place the paper pattern so the point is at the center point of the folded cloth and pin in place. Cut out the fabric around the pattern curve.

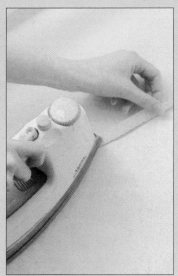

4 Unfold the cloth and press. Machine stitch around the cloth ¾ inch from the raw edge of the fabric. This line of stitching (shown here in a contrasting color to make it visible) forms the hemline.

5 Turn up the hem allowance and press to form a crisp edge. The stitching should roll over naturally to the wrong side to create a clean edge. Turn under half the hem allowance and press again.

6 Pin the hem in place and baste if you wish. Stitch by machine just inside the folded edge. Alternatively, stitch by hand for a nearly invisible finish. Remove any remaining pins or basting and press.

DECORATING WITH DISTINCT STYLE

Combine a few favorite accessories with just the right colors to define your most personal room.

VARIATIONS ON A THEME

Fresh Mix

• A contemporary room features streamlined shapes and touchable textures like the waffle-weave **button-together pillows** (page 130). Gentle tones of cream and beige keep the room light and restful.

• **Tone-on-tone** (page 132) stripes offer subtle definition to the walls while keeping the mood restful.

• Simple **tab-top curtains** (page 134) mimic the clean lines of the walls and always look fresh and modern.

• A **simple shelf** (page 136) on brackets serves as a photo gallery for black-and-white and sepia-toned photographs.

Shaker Simplicity

• Here, the clean, spare lines of Shaker-inspired furniture showcase the natural beauty of wood. Another plus: flat-fronted drawers thwart dust.

• Freedom from clutter is a basic tenet of this style.

• A signature Shaker detail, the rail outfitted with dozens of wooden pegs, circles the room and offers opportunities for practical storage and attractive display.

Romantic Setting

• A richly layered decorating scheme pairs bold floral prints and neat stripes with dark wood furniture to evoke the romantic Victorian mood.

• Liberal splashes of white in the bedding and the woodwork balance the heaviness of the more formal fabrics.

• Piles of pillows bespeak relaxation and comfort. Maximize the prettiness by dressing up **pillow cases** (page 138) of your own.

Cottage Coziness

• Coordinate pastels and whites for an airy country bedroom. Pure white furniture looks clean and bright against the rosy glow of the walls. Bare wood floors lend a light, summery feel all year long.

• The lace table runner, tacked in place with whimsical crescent moons, becomes an improvised window valance.

• A simple **grapevine wreath** (page 140), a watering can wall decoration and the birdhouse on the floor serve as rustic reminders of the country cottage theme.

BUTTON-TOGETHER PILLOW COVERS

Cleverly buttoned pillow covers make an attractive addition to any decor.

YOU WILL NEED

- ❏ 18-INCH SQUARE PILLOW FORM
- ❏ FOUR 21- BY 15-INCH PIECES OF FABRIC
- ❏ SIX 1-INCH DECORATIVE BUTTONS
- ❏ TAPE MEASURE
- ❏ PINS & SEAM RIPPER
- ❏ CHALK PENCIL
- ❏ SEWING MACHINE
- ❏ THREAD & NEEDLE
- ❏ SHEARS
- ❏ IRON

BEFORE YOU BEGIN

Great fabrics combine with decorative buttons for a unique pillow cover.

Cutting and Marking

For an 18-inch pillow, cut two fabric pieces of one color 21 by 13 inches and two pieces of a different color 21 by 14½ inches. These measurements allow for a 1½-inch-wide band for the 1-inch buttons and buttonholes.

- For variation, each pillow cover half can be made of different fabric colors or patterns.
- To match patterned fabrics, cut all four pieces in the same direction.

Measuring for Buttonholes

To determine buttonhole length, measure the width of the button, then add the button's depth for buttoning ease. This total equals the buttonhole length. When using buttons with a shank, do not include the shank in the depth measurement.

To mark buttonhole placement, find center of band (right). Measure from seam to seam to find center of band length and across band from folded edge to stitching to find center of band width; mark. To mark center for remaining buttonholes, find center from mark to seams. Mark beginning and end of each buttonhole by centering buttonhole length, calculated above, on each mark.

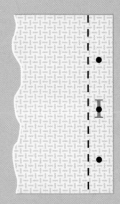

Button Pillow Options

Mother of pearl buttons dress up this linen pillow cover (left). For a different look, the width of the buttonhole band is ¼ inch narrower than the button diameter.

These bright, soft pillow covers (right) enliven a child's room. The buttonhole bands are off-center for a fun twist.

MAKING BUTTONED PILLOW COVERS

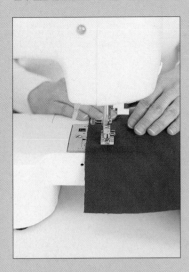

1 With right sides together, match short sides and long sides of fabric (Before you Begin). Stitch 1-inch seams on both short sides, but only one long side of each pillow cover half. Trim corners and press seams open.

2 Make buttonhole and button bands on open ends of each pillow cover half. Turn under 1½ inches and again 1½ inches; pin. Stitch close to inner fold; press.

3 On right side of smaller pillow cover, mark three buttonholes with chalk pencil, centering them on the band (Before you Begin). Turn pillow cover over and mark three more buttonholes on other side.

4 Following instructions in your sewing machine manual, make buttonhole at each mark. Clip thread and slit open buttonholes with fine-pointed scissors or seam ripper.

5 Slip both pillow cover halves over pillow form, overlapping band with buttonholes over band without buttonholes. Using tailor's chalk, mark button placement on button band. Remove pillow cover from form and hand stitch buttons at marks. Button pillow cover halves together over form. Mix and match cover halves to create different looks.

TONE-ON-TONE PAINTED WALLS

Patterns painted with polyurethane add subtle dimension to walls.

YOU WILL NEED

- ❏ POLYURETHANE
- ❏ PENCIL
- ❏ CHALK LINE & TACK
- ❏ SPONGE BRUSH
- ❏ PAINTER'S MASKING TAPE
- ❏ TAPE MEASURE
- ❏ CLEAN CLOTH
- ❏ SMALL PAINTBRUSH

BEFORE YOU BEGIN

Whatever pattern you select, the technique remains the same. The effects, however, can dramatically change the style and feel of a room.

Choosing the Perfect Pattern

Classic stripes in varying widths create the unmistakable look of traditional wallpaper (right). No matter how subtle, polyurethane stripes direct your eye lengthwise along the wall, producing the illusion of high ceilings.

Whimsical stencils resembling cartoon symbols enliven the surface of an otherwise plain accent wall (right). Polyurethane designs add a hint of pattern to a decorating scheme without overpowering the room.

A timeless harlequin pattern dresses up the walls (right), giving a room of simple furnishings a fresh look. Both direct and indirect lighting will enhance the subtle contrast between the glossy and matte diamonds.

Design Ideas

Use your decor as a springboard to painted polyurethane designs.
• Imitate the patterns in plaid upholstery by crisscrossing pieces of tape on the wall.
• Highlight a particular theme, such as sports or gardening, by stenciling related motifs.
• Contrast sleek, modern furnishings with a busy geometric design made by drawing a simple grid on the wall.

CREATING A PATTERN WITH POLYURETHANE

1 Lightly mark every 6 inches along top and bottom edges of wall. Working from right edge, tack chalk line to first top mark, then pull down to second mark from right. Continue across wall. Reverse; work from left to right.

2 When harlequin pattern is completely marked, apply painter's masking tape along inside line of diamonds in alternating rows. Cut tape edges diagonally to fit. Wipe away chalk lines before continuing.

3 Use sponge brush to paint exposed diamonds with polyurethane. Paint one row completely across wall before painting next row of exposed diamonds. Immediately wipe drips with clean cloth.

HANDY HINTS

Because a flat finish paint decreases the visual flaws on a wall, the base color should be painted in a flat or eggshell finish, while the patterns and designs should be painted with glossy polyurethane.

For a shimmering, translucent finish, add a small amount of colored paint or metallic glaze to the polyurethane.

Avoid uneven edges by pressing the masking tape firmly against the wall with your fingertips.

TAKE NOTE

Be sure to wipe away any chalk lines before you begin painting. Chalk lines will be permanently visible if you do not remove them.

On a newly painted wall, wait until the paint cures (2 to 4 weeks) before using tape to mark patterns. If the base paint has not completely cured, paint may pull away from the wall when you remove the tape.

4 When polyurethane is thoroughly dry, gently lift masking tape from wall. Be careful not to pull too hard; otherwise, tape's adhesive might remove paint. If necessary, use small paintbrush to touch up polyurethane diamonds or painted background.

TAB-TOP CURTAINS

A modern approach to curtains, fabric loops work with any room's style.

You Will Need

- ❏ CURTAIN ROD
- ❏ CURTAIN FABRIC
- ❏ NEEDLE & THREAD
- ❏ FABRIC SHEARS
- ❏ TAPE MEASURE
- ❏ STRAIGHT PINS
- ❏ SEWING MACHINE
- ❏ IRON

BEFORE YOU BEGIN

Stitch loops into a seam at the top of the curtain, raw edges covered by the facing fabric. Stitch the side seams and hems before you begin.

Figuring the Fabric

Follow these steps to determine how much fabric you will need.
- For length of main panel, measure distance from the bottom of the curtain rod to the hem position. Add 4 inches for the hem.
- Measure the length of the rod and divide by two to find the width for each curtain panel.
- Multiply the width of each curtain panel by 1½ to allow fullness for the curtains to drape. Then add 3 inches to each side for the hems.
- Allow extra width for seams if the fabric needs to be pieced.

- A strip of fabric 6 inches deep (the facing) runs across the back of the top of the curtain. Allow 1 inch at each end for hems.
- For each tab, cut a strip 9 inches wide and 11 inches long.

To calculate number of tabs, measure width of curtain. The tabs should be positioned 4 to 6 inches apart (below). For a single width of curtain fabric, plan at least five tabs.

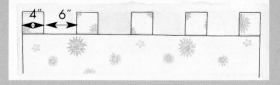

Sewing the Curtains

To sew the curtains, make a 1½-inch double fold down each side edge and press. Stitch by machine or hand. Turn up and fold 1 inch and then 3 inches across the lower edge of curtain for hem and press. Stitch by hand, turning in and trimming corners to reduce bulk (right).

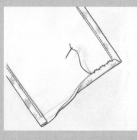

FINISHING TAB-TOP CURTAINS

DOLLAR SENSE

Tab-tops can be used to shorten or lengthen existing curtains. To make curtains slightly longer, undo the heading and press out. Then add tabs and a facing in a coordinating color. To shorten the curtains, use the extra fabric from the curtains to make the tabs.

1 Cut a piece of fabric 2 inches wider than finished curtain and about 6 inches deep. Turn under a 1-inch single hem along lower edge and down each short side. Press, tucking in corners for a neat miter. Stitch by machine.

2 For each tab, cut a strip of fabric 9 inches wide by 11 inches. Fold in half lengthwise, right sides together, and stitch, making ½-inch seams. Press seams open, then turn right side out. Refold fabric so seams are in the center. Press.

3 Lay out the main panel of the curtain right side up. Position the folded tabs, seam inside, across the top edge so that the raw edges match. Check that the tabs are evenly spaced. Pin in place.

4 Position the facing over the tabs, right sides together, so that the raw edge of the facing is about ½ inch below the top of the curtain and the raw edges of the tabs. Check that the tabs are straight, and pin the facing in position.

5 Baste along the top edge of the facing, ½ inch from the raw edge. Stitch the facing in place by machine. Press the stitching. Then turn the facing to the wrong side of the curtain so that the tabs stand up.

6 Press the facing to the fabric. Slipstitch the turned-under ends of the facing in place just inside the outer edge of the curtain, and slipstitch the lower edge of the facing to the curtain so that the stitches do not show on the right side. Insert the curtain rod through the tab tops to hang. Then pull back both curtain panels to the sides with matching tiebacks.

SIMPLE STORAGE SHELF

This versatile shelf can offer a tidy storage solution that fits any decor.

YOU WILL NEED

- ❏ TWO 30-INCH-LONG PIECES OF 1X8 CLEAR PINE
- ❏ WOOD GLUE
- ❏ CLAMPS
- ❏ HAMMER & NAILS
- ❏ DECORATIVE BRACKETS & HOOKS
- ❏ DRILL, SCREWS & SCREWDRIVER
- ❏ WOOD STAIN OR PAINT
- ❏ FOAM BRUSH
- ❏ TAPE MEASURE OR RULER

BEFORE YOU BEGIN

You can easily change the look and cost of this uncomplicated carpentry project by your choice of brackets and hooks.

Brackets

Fake stone: You may be lucky enough to find wonderful antique plaster brackets in a salvage yard or at a tag sale. However, it is very simple and far more inexpensive to fake the look of stone or marble (right). Just purchase a wooden bracket, either plain or embossed with fancy scrollwork, and then finish with special stone-texture spray paint topped with a clear matte finish.

Wrought Iron: In their most basic form, wrought iron brackets evoke 18th century blacksmith shop simplicity, while more ornate curlicues recall Victorian splendor. Wrought iron brackets are available in most hardware stores (below).

Wood: Unadorned wooden brackets can be an economical choice (right). Stain them the same color as the shelves so they are unobtrusive, or paint the shelf and brackets in two different, bright colors for eye-catching attention.

Hooks

- Coat hooks offer an endless variety of style, material, color and cost. Some types to consider: wrought iron, ceramic, wood and brass.
- Do not limit yourself to actual hooks. Items such as antique, spindle-style doorstops, door knobs or drawer pulls are excellent alternatives.
- Consider function when selecting coat hooks. Knobbed wooden pegs may look good, but bulky coats might fall off unless curved hooks are used.

BUILDING THE SHELF

1 Sand the ends of the boards. Run wood glue along one long edge of one board. Attach the second board lengthwise at a right angle to the first board. Clamp in place until the glue dries. Reinforce the joint with finishing nails.

2 Position the brackets into the right angles on the shelf's underside, making sure the brackets are flush with the edges of the wood. Mark screw holes with pencil and drill starter holes. Screw the brackets into the wood shelving.

3 Using a foam brush, apply stain to wood. There is no need to stain the back of the unit, as this will be attached to the wall. Let the stain dry thoroughly and then sand lightly. Apply a second coat of stain and let it dry completely.

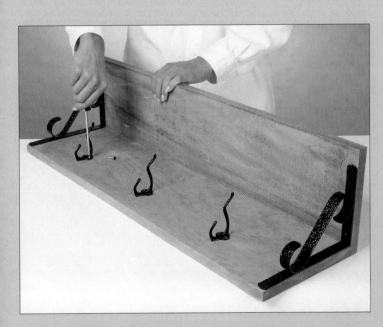

4 Measure and mark the placement of the coat hooks so that they are evenly spaced. Drill starter holes and screw in the hooks. Locate wall studs and then drill pilot holes into the shelf beside the decorative brackets; screw the shelf to the wall.

DRESSED-UP PILLOWCASES

Give plain pillowcases a designer touch with innovative edgings.

BEFORE YOU BEGIN

Adding beautiful trim or elegant fabric can turn a plain pillowcase into a treasured heirloom.

Elegant Trims

Different types of trims can be sewn to pillowcases to create various effects.

- Apply lace trim, flat or pre-gathered, for a romantic effect (1).
- Damask, a closely woven fabric with a tone-on-tone jacquard pattern, adds sophistication (2).
- For a delicate touch, use tulle or handkerchief linen with a woven hem pattern (3), a handkerchief that has been monogrammed (4) or lace cut on a diagonal.

Trimming the Pillowcase

1 With a seam ripper, open pillowcase seam 2 inches past piping. Remove hem stitches and piping. Piping stitching line, which will be used as a cutting guide, remains visible until after laundering process.

2 Cut away hem section, which will be referred to as hem panel, along piping stitching line. Turn long, bottom edge of hem panel under ½ inch; press. Fold handkerchief in half diagonally; finger press.

3 Cut handkerchief in half along diagonal marking. Center handkerchief along edge of pillowcase top. Pin with wrong side of handkerchief against right side of pillowcase. Stitch with ¼-inch seam.

4 With right sides together and handkerchief sandwiched between, pin unfolded edge of hem panel to pillowcase. Sew with ¼-inch seam. Machine zigzag this seam to prevent fraying.

5 Press seam flat toward fabric. Fold hem panel to inside of pillowcase. Stitch hem panel to pillowcase along pressed edge of hem panel, taking care not to catch handkerchief in sewing.

6 With right sides together, sew open edge of the pillowcase closed with a ¼-inch seam. Backstitch at outer edge to add strength and to avoid tearing when pillowcase is pulled over pillow.

7 Turn pillowcase right side out. Pin handkerchief in place through top layer only, keeping it flat. Hand stitch invisibly along outer edge of handkerchief to secure it. Do not pull or distort shape of handkerchief.

GRAPEVINE HYDRANGEA WREATH

Gather favorite garden blooms to make a timeless dried wreath.

YOU WILL NEED

❏ 18-INCH GRAPEVINE WREATH BASE
❏ ASSORTED HYDRANGEA BLOOMS
❏ GLUE GUN & GLUE STICKS
❏ SCISSORS
❏ FRENCH WIRED RIBBON
❏ FLORIST'S WIRE
❏ FLORAL SEALER

BEFORE YOU BEGIN

To make a long-lasting hydrangea wreath, select plump, mature blossoms and dry them slowly.

Preparing Flowers

Pick hydrangea clusters in late summer or early fall when they are mature and the petals feel slightly firm and leathery. If you pick them too early, they will shrivel up rather than dry naturally.

• To air dry them, place the branches upright in a tall, waterless vase, leaving them to dry for several days.
• Another drying method is to place the blooms with their stems upright in a container with 2 inches of water (above right). Leave them to dry for at least two days after the water evaporates.
• During the drying phase, keep the plant materials in a cool, dry place that has good circulation. Keep sunlight exposure to a minimum to preserve the hydrangeas' beautiful color.
• When you are ready to make the wreath, you must first snip the clusters from the stems. Using sharp shears, trim off all but one inch of the stems, and lay the clusters, faceup, on a flat, clean surface.

Hydrangea Colors

Colors vary considerably according to plant variety and soil conditions.
• The favorite white "hills of snow" dry to a pale tan or green. Peegee hydrangeas, also white, dry to pinkish-gold.
• Bigleaf hydrangeas, ranging from blue to pink when fresh, dry to pale versions of the same.
• For variation, add blue and pink color to blooming hydrangea by changing the acidity of the soil. For blue tones, add aluminum sulfate to the soil. For pink tones, add lime to the soil.

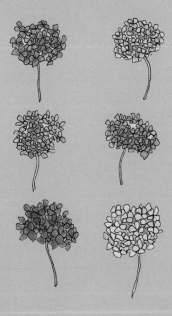

Making a Hydrangea Wreath

1 Lay grapevine wreath base and a collection of dried blooms of variegated colors on your work surface. Gently separate the extra large blooms into smaller, more manageable tufts.

2 Apply glue to the underside of the first cluster. Beginning at 8 o'clock on the wreath, gently press the cluster against the grapevine base until it holds. Place tufts close to one another to cover the base.

3 The flowers may shrink slightly with time, so be generous in the application of blossoms. Proceed around the wreath until you have reached 4 o'clock. When finished, go back to fill in any areas, if necessary.

4 Cut a 3-yard length of French wired ribbon. Hold the ribbon tight between thumb and forefinger and begin to gather it into generous loops. Twist as you make each return to keep the ribbon right side up.

5 Attach the bow to the grapevine with florist's wire at 2 o'clock for a casual and charming effect. Once the bow is attached, add a dab of hot glue to the underside of the bow for reinforcement. Spray the entire wreath with a floral sealer to preserve its beauty.

DECORATING WITH SHEETS

Transform ordinary bed linens into attractive, soft furnishings throughout your home.

MAKING IT WORK

Available in a variety of coordinated patterns, bed linens offer economical and easy-sew alternatives to yard goods.

Clean Finish

• Creating slipcovers, **futon covers** (page 144) and other fabric accessories from sheets holds the distinct advantage of allowing you to work with wide material that comes already hemmed or selvage-finished on four sides.

• To improvise a slipcover, drape the sofa with one or two sheets and tuck them in neatly all around. Sew a separate dust ruffle with an elasticized casing big enough to skirt the entire couch. Use adhesive hook-and-loop fastener tape in spots, if necessary, to keep the ruffle in place.

• Make a **lamp cover-up** (page 146) with linen matching the pillows, tying the fabric at the top of the base with tasseled cording.

• Cover throw pillows with coordinating fabrics, taking advantage of the piped edges of pillowcases and flat sheets.

• When substituting sheets for 60-inch-wide fabric, note that a twin sheet equals almost 3 yards, full equals 3½ yards, queen equals 4¼ yards and king equals 5 yards.

• Set a pretty table cover on the diagonal to enhance the table's natural beauty while protecting the hardworking center.

VARIATIONS ON A THEME

Country Bedroom

• Sew a **duvet cover** (page 148) from bold printed sheets, placed back-to-back. Enhance the look with a reversible throw and a mix of square, flanged, ruffled and bolster pillows, all sewn from coordinating linens.

• A box-pleated bed skirt adds a simple, tailored note among frills.

• Use coordinating bed linens to make **tent flap curtains** (page 150) that add style and flair to your decor.

Decorative Dining

• **Seat cushions** (page 152) and place mats, sewn from a sunny, floral sheet, add to the warmth of the room. Make a supply of fabric napkins by hemming 18-inch squares from the extra linens.

• To make piped edging for seat covers, seam together 2-inch-wide bias strips cut from sheets and fold lengthwise around purchased cording; stitch close to cording.

• Trim a sideboard **table runner** (page 154) with stripes and taper it to a point for a dramatic finish.

Bathroom Beauty

• Layer florals with crisp, striped sheeting to create an elegant **shower curtain** (page 156). Linens made from cotton and polyester blends ensure the brightest colors in a range of patterns.

• Striped valances cap off the window and shower curtain. The large hem of a flat sheet doubles as a ready-made curtain rod pocket. For a ruffled top, sew a seam in the center of the hem to make two channels.

• Use cafe curtains, twin panels cut from a vivid sheet of orange, to balance privacy and light.

CUSTOM-FIT FUTON COVERS

Update your futon with a quick-stitch cushion cover.

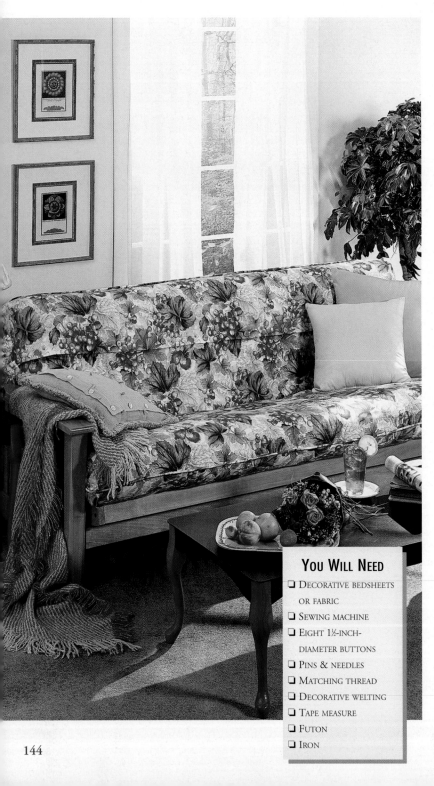

BEFORE YOU BEGIN

Accent the cover with corded edging. Piece 2-inch-wide fabric bias strips together to make a continuous strip, fold in half and stitch cording inside.

Cutting Fabric

You will need to cut three separate pieces for each cushion cover.

• For the back panel, calculate the width of the panel by adding the width (a) and the depth (c) measurements of the futon cushion together, plus 1 inch. For the panel length, add the length (b) and the depth (c) measurements together, plus 1 inch. Cut out.

• For the top panel, measure and cut a piece of fabric the same width as the back panel. For the length, add the depth and three-quarters the length of the cushion, plus 3½ inches.

• For the top flap, measure and cut a piece of fabric the same width as the back panel. For the length, add the depth and one-quarter the length of the cushion, plus 3½ inches.

• Sew the panels together with a ½-inch seam allowance.

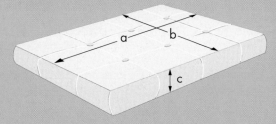

Custom-Fit Corners

Create a custom fit by cutting and stitching the corners of the futon cushion cover. Begin by folding one corner of the front panel diagonally so that right sides are facing. Measure and cut a diagonal line across the corner that equals one-half the depth (c) of the futon cushion. Repeat for the remaining corners on the front and back panels.

Trim all seams at the corners to keep the fabric from bunching together.

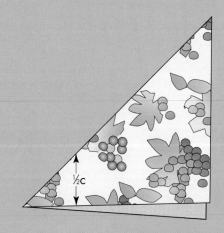

Sewing a Fold-Over Cushion Cover

1 Turn one long edge of flap under ½ inch, then 2½ inches and press. Topstitch along fold, ¼ inch from edge. Repeat for top edge of front panel. Machine-stitch 8 buttonholes evenly along top of flap, 1 inch from finished edge.

2 Lay top panel and flap over back panel, right sides up, so stitched edge of flap overlaps stitched edge of top panel. Align top edges with length of back panel. Pin top panel and flap at sides to make front panel; stitch.

3 Create a custom-fit cover by diagonally folding, marking and then stitching each corner of the panels together (Before you Begin). Trim excess fabric from seam allowances to prevent bunching.

4 Lay back panel right side up on a flat surface. With raw edges aligned, pin welting to back panel. Clip welting seams around curves so it will lay flat. Overlap ends of welting. Using a zipper foot, stitch in place.

5 Using a zipper foot and with right sides facing and raw edges aligned, pin and stitch front and back panels together. Follow stitching line of welting. Clip curves and trim threads. Turn cover right side out.

6 Lay cushion cover on a flat surface and press. Mark button placement on front panel underneath buttonholes. Using matching thread, attach buttons to cover. Insert futon cushion and button cover in place.

FABRIC COVER-UPS FOR LAMPS

Create a new look for a lamp by covering the lamp base with fabric.

YOU WILL NEED

❑ LAMP
❑ FABRIC
❑ LINING FABRIC
❑ DECORATIVE CORDING
❑ SEWING MACHINE
❑ SEWING THREAD
❑ IRON
❑ PENCIL & MARKER
❑ STRING
❑ PAPER

BEFORE YOU BEGIN

While cover-ups work best when placed over a ginger jar lamp, they can also be used to cover table lamps with rectangular or square bases.

Measuring the Lamp

To create a pattern for the cover-up, measure the lamp being decorated.

• Determine the lamp measurement (a+b+c) for the fabric cover-up: Measure from the neck of one side of the lamp base, down (a) and across the base bottom (b) and up the opposite side of the lamp (c).

• To the lamp measurement, add 7 inches for the ruffle and the seam allowance and 1½ inches for the casing. This takes into account the full diameter of the cover-up (below).

• For the lining and face fabric, purchase squares of fabric the size of the cover-up diameter. If the fabric is narrower than this diameter, you will need to piece it.

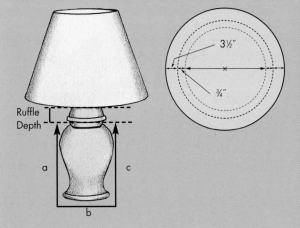

Creating a Pattern

Cut a square of craft paper to the size of the cover-up diameter. Fold paper in half, and then in half again, to make a smaller square.

Tie a piece of string to a pencil. Measuring from the pencil, mark the string at half the cover-up diameter. Hold the string mark on the folded corner of the paper and draw an arc.

Carefully cut along the arc through all the layers of paper to make the cover-up pattern. Unfold the paper and press it flat.

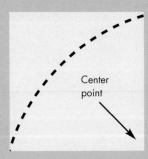

Center point

Making a Fabric Cover-Up

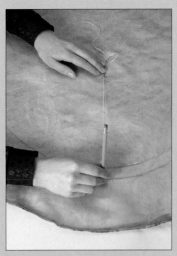

1 Transfer pattern (Before you Begin) to fabric; cut out. Repeat for lining fabric. With right sides together and raw edges aligned, stitch fabrics together with ½-inch seam, leaving a 6-inch opening. Clip curves close to seam.

2 Turn cover-up right side out and slipstitch opening closed. Press flat. Position lamp in center of fabric and mark electrical cord placement with marker. Make a 1½-inch buttonhole at placement mark.

3 Starting at the center, use half the lamp measurement (Before you Begin) to mark the first casing circle with pencil and string. Make second circle ¾ inch beyond first. Machine-stitch over both casing lines.

HANDY HINTS

Choose coordinating fabrics for the lining and front of the cover so that, if desired, the cover-up can be reversed.

DOLLAR SENSE

Use scraps of fabric left over from pillows, comforters or other fabric accessories in a room to make a lamp cover-up. Scraps of cording and trim can be used for the tie.

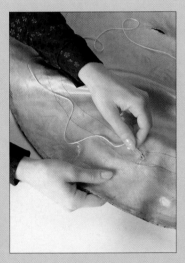

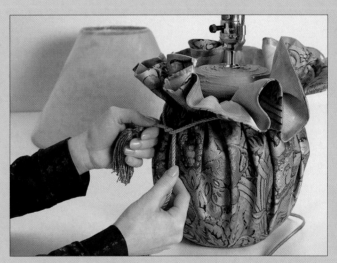

4 Cut small opening in lining fabric casing. Cut 36-inch piece of string and attach one end to safety pin. Thread safety pin through casing around entire circle. Pull string through small opening in lining fabric.

5 Position lamp in center of fabric cover-up, pulling electrical cord through buttonhole. Pull cover-up over sides of lamp so that casing fits around top of lamp base. Pull string taut and tie to secure.

6 Tuck casing string ends to inside. Adjust fabric so that gathers lay smooth and flat around lamp. Position ruffles so that lining and outside of cover-up alternately show. For finishing touch, tie ribbon or decorative cord around outside of casing.

QUICK-SEW DUVET COVERS

Protect your duvet with a colorful cover sewn from two sheets.

BEFORE YOU BEGIN

Several different styles of duvets are available. Weigh price against durability to choose the best one for you.

Selecting a Duvet to Cover

• A duvet, sometimes called a comforter, can last a lifetime. Buy one made from a cotton fabric or a cotton and synthetic blend to ensure lasting durability and washability.
• Originally from Europe, good-down duvets are con- sidered the ultimate in luxury; however, they are also very expensive. Many duvets today are filled with a down and feather combination. Or for those with allergies, synthetic and wool versions are available.

More stitching is needed to minimize the shifting of down or the bunching of synthetic filling. Look for horizontal and vertical stitching in square patterns for the best buy (right).

A lightweight duvet, for use during warmer months, holds less filling than winter-weight duvets. The stitching on lightweight duvets often follows a straight parallel line called baffling (right).

A tacked or tied assembly is sometimes used to secure a layer of synthetic batting (right). This method is not usually used with down or feathers, since they shift so easily during laundering.

SEWING A DUVET COVER

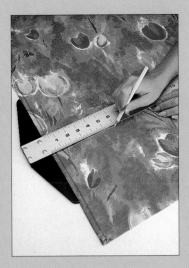

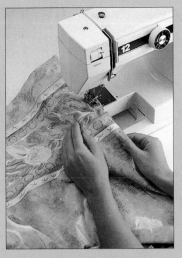

1 To find cutting width and length, measure the duvet. Add 2 inches to width and 4½ inches to length. Using a yardstick and a T square, measure the cutting dimensions, mark right-angled corners and cut two sheets to measure.

2 With right sides facing and all edges even, pin the sheets together along the top and two sides. Stitch along the three edges with a ½-inch seam allowance. Pivot and turn at the corners.

3 To prevent the seams from fraying, clean finish the edges by stitching a second row of stitches ¼ inch from the first. Trim fabric close to the second row of stitching and clip at corners.

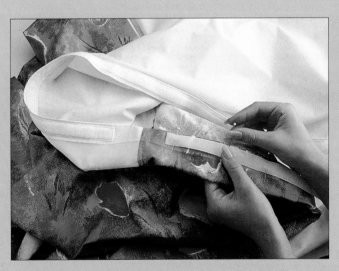

4 Slide cover onto ironing board and press seams to one side. On unstitched edge, fold up 1 inch to wrong side and press. Again fold 1 inch and press in place to create a 1-inch double fold hem.

5 Cut hook-and-loop fastener tape 2 inches shorter than width of cover. Open out inside fold of hem. Center and pin each half of tape to top and bottom of cover between folds of hem. Stitch tape to hem on long sides.

6 Refold hem and pin. For the top of the cover or for a reversible cover, stitch close to the fold with a blind hem stitch. For linings, topstitch close to the fold. Turn duvet cover right side out. Slip cover over duvet and fasten the hook-and-loop fastener tape.

TENT FLAP CURTAINS

Give curtains graphic appeal by hanging them to open like a tent.

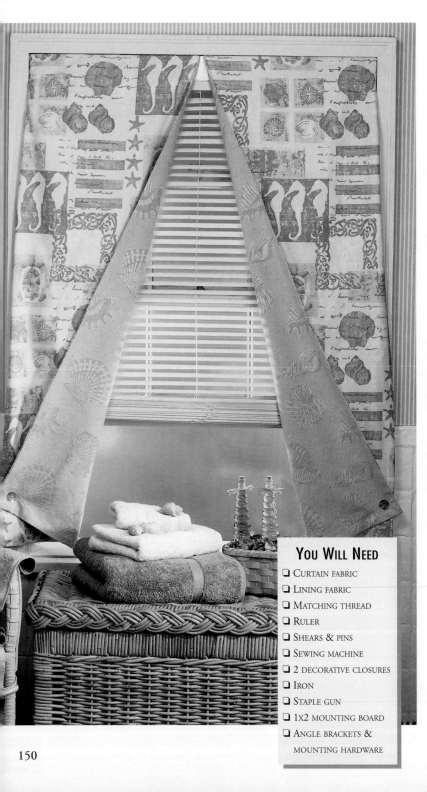

YOU WILL NEED

- ❏ CURTAIN FABRIC
- ❏ LINING FABRIC
- ❏ MATCHING THREAD
- ❏ RULER
- ❏ SHEARS & PINS
- ❏ SEWING MACHINE
- ❏ 2 DECORATIVE CLOSURES
- ❏ IRON
- ❏ STAPLE GUN
- ❏ 1x2 MOUNTING BOARD
- ❏ ANGLE BRACKETS & MOUNTING HARDWARE

BEFORE YOU BEGIN

Choose lining fabric and a tieback design that complements the curtain style and your room's décor.

Figuring Measurements

Measure length and width of window inside window frame.

• To work out dimensions for fabric, divide window width in half, then add 1¼ inches for cutting width. Add 3⅛ inches to length to achieve cutting length of each panel.

• Cut exact size panels for lining.

• For mounting board, cut a 1x2 board the same length as the width of the window. If curtain panels are to hang flush with front of window frame, trim depth of board to same depth as window frame.

Tieback Alternatives

Affix the tiebacks midway down the window frame.

• Attach a grommet halfway down the inside edge of each curtain panel.

• Secure plain cup hooks at corresponding points on the window frame.

• Another option is to thread a gold or brass beaded chain through the grommet, and attach the chain to a decorative hook mounted on the frame.

Instead of using a mounting board, construct a rod pocket casing along the top edge of each narrow curtain panel, and hang the curtains from a rod above the window frame.

• Use a narrow strip of face or lining fabric to make a fabric loop.

• Catch the strip ends in the seam to create a loop long enough to drape over a decorative hook mounted on the wall at the loops' level.

Making the Curtains

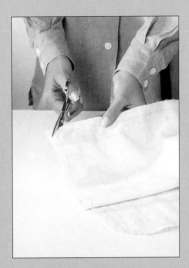

1 Cut fabric and lining panels to appropriate length and width (Before you Begin). With right sides together, sew lining to fabric at sides and bottom, using ½-inch seam allowance. Clip bottom corners to reduce bulk. Turn panels right side out.

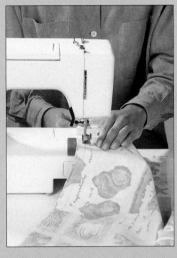

2 On right side, press panel carefully, taking care that lining does not roll toward right side of panel. Stitch top edge ⅝ inch from raw edge. Top edge can remain unfinished since it will not be visible.

3 Determine placement of buttonhole at lower inside corner of panel. Make buttonholes. Sew buttons to right outer edge of panel.

HANDY HINTS

Select fabrics with enough body to hold the shape and position of the tent flap opening. Heavy cotton, linen and decorating fabrics are good choices.

OOPS

If you are not satisfied with the position of the flap opening, remove the button and reposition the flaps as desired; keep in mind that the buttonhole is permanent. Resew the button in a different position.

4 Mark a line at center of mounting board to ensure even placement of panels. If desired, paint or cover board with fabric, since center may be visible when hanging.

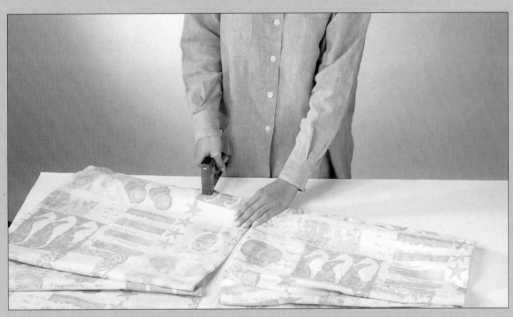

5 Staple top edge of panels to top rear of mounting board, beginning at center and working toward ends of board. Be sure inside edges of curtain panels meet at center of mounting board. Use angle brackets to hang board inside window frame. Button flaps open.

TAILOR-MADE SEAT CUSHIONS

Piping defines the edging lines so seat cushions look tailor-made.

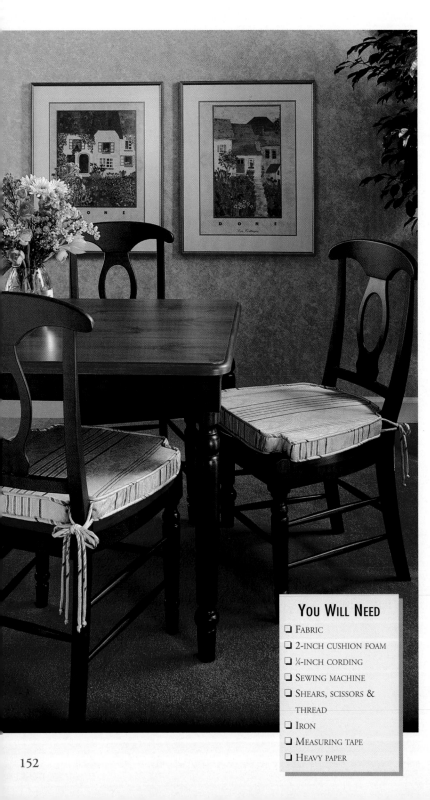

BEFORE YOU BEGIN

Purchase 2-inch-thick foam from an upholstery or craft store for cushions. Cut out fabric following a paper pattern.

Cutting Out a Pattern

Measure the widest part of the seat, both the length and the width. Cut a piece of scrap paper to this size. Place it on the chair and use a pencil to mark any curved or angled edges. Cut out the traced pattern (right).

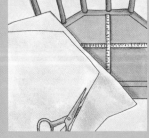

Fold pattern in half lengthwise to make sure both sides are equal. This is particularly important so that the cushion can be reversed, top to bottom. Make any necessary changes to ensure pattern fits perfectly (right).

Cutting Fabric to Fit

Determine amount of fabric needed, buying extra for pattern repeats and piping if necessary. Position pattern over fabric in desired placement. Pin in place and cut out fabric, adding ½ inch for seams on all sides.

Creating Side Panel and Piping

Cut 3-inch-wide strips for seat cushion sides. This side panel is called a boxing strip.
• One long strip matches pattern at front of cushion and is long enough to wrap around two sides. One short strip matches pattern at back and overlaps first strip by ½ inch at each end.

• Make fabric-covered piping. Cut 1½-inch-wide strips along fabric bias—diagonal to the grain. Join strips together with ½-inch seams. Wrap bias fabric right side out around ¼-inch cording. Stitch close to the cording with a zipper foot. Cut edge to ½ inch wide.

YOU WILL NEED
- ❑ FABRIC
- ❑ 2-INCH CUSHION FOAM
- ❑ ¼-INCH CORDING
- ❑ SEWING MACHINE
- ❑ SHEARS, SCISSORS & THREAD
- ❑ IRON
- ❑ MEASURING TAPE
- ❑ HEAVY PAPER

SEWING A PIPED SEAT CUSHION

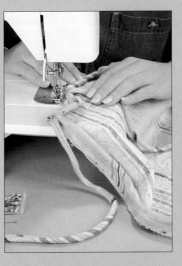

HANDY HINTS

An electric knife cuts through foam like butter! It is the easiest tool to use for a clean cut through foam.

TAKE NOTE

Spray a **protective** coating on cushion fabric to prevent permanent stains.

1 Pin the piping to the right side of top cushion fabric, keeping the raw edges even. Overlap piping ends at back of cushion. Stitch a ½-inch seam. Stitch piping in same manner to fabric for bottom of cushion.

2 Cut 1½-inch-wide fabric strips 24 inches long for ties. Fold lengthwise; stitch ½-inch seam along long edge and one end; trim edges. Using a safety pin, turn tie right side out. Sew in place on both cushion pieces.

3 Sew boxing strips, right sides together and with ½-inch seams, to form band. Make sure the boxing strip fits the cushion size and that the pattern on the strip matches up with the front of seat.

4 Pin the boxing strip to the top cushion fabric, right sides together. Stitch in place using the piping and cushion seam as a guide. Keep the new stitching just inside this guideline so it doesn't show on outside.

5 Repeat Step 4, attaching boxing strip to the bottom cushion fabric. Leave an opening to insert the foam.

6 Clip seams at corners and curves. Press seams toward the boxing strip. Turn cushion case right side out. Insert foam cushion cut to size. Then slipstitch cushion cover closed.

Colorful Table Runner

A table runner adds color, texture and style to a dining table.

BEFORE YOU BEGIN

Use a table runner over a complementary tablecloth, or by itself to highlight a table's natural beauty.

Pattern-Making and Cutting

For a table runner 70 inches long and 18 inches wide, refer to the illustration (below) for making paper pattern pieces. Remember to add ½-inch seam allowances to all sides of each of these patterns.

• Draw a rectangle 70 inches by 18 inches; draw second rectangle 64 inches by 12 inches centered inside first. Then draw a diagonal line from each outer corner to each inner corner.

• Outside pieces 1, 2, 3 and 4 create the frame. Center piece 5 is the main piece of the table runner.

• Cut along each marked line to create pattern pieces. Add ½-inch seam allowances around all edges of each pattern piece.

• Pieces 2 and 4 require piecing to obtain correct length. Cut one each of pieces 1, 2, 3 and 4 from contrast fabric. If you are using a striped contrast fabric, match edges of stripes at short ends of strips. This will create a professional-looking chevron effect at the corners when strips are sewn together.

• Cut piece 5 from main fabric.

• Cut one rectangle 71 inches by 19 inches from contrast fabric for lining side of runner.

• Cut one rectangular piece of batting, 71 inches by 19 inches.

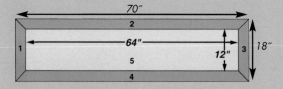

Interlinings

An interlining, a layer of fabric sandwiched between the lining and the main fabric, will add body to the table runner and protect the table from heat and moisture.

• Polyester fleece or needle-punched batting are suitable interlinings because they retain their shape through repeated laundering.

• A piece of flannel will add support without stiffness. A thin polyester quilt batting is also good.

YOU WILL NEED

❑ 2 YARDS FABRIC
❑ 2¼ YARDS CONTRAST FABRIC
❑ THREAD
❑ 2 YARDS THIN BATTING
❑ SEWING MACHINE
❑ IRON
❑ SHEARS & SCISSORS
❑ NEEDLES, PINS & SAFETY PINS

SEWING A TABLE RUNNER

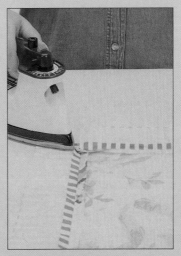

1 Join all four outside pieces to form frame as shown (Before you Begin). Stitch short diagonal ends, right sides together, matching fabric pattern. Trim edges; press seam allowances open.

2 With right sides together, pin inside edge of frame piece to outside edge of main piece with short sides and long sides matching. Make sure corners are aligned. Stitch carefully, pivoting exactly at corners.

3 Trim seam allowances to ¼ inch and clip corners diagonally. Press seams open, carefully pressing corner seam allowances flat. Cut lining fabric, piecing if necessary. Place face down on a flat surface.

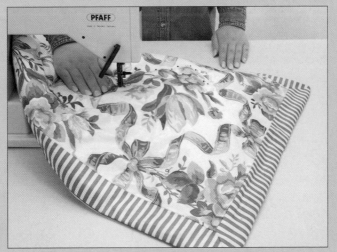

4 Hand- or machine-baste batting to wrong side of lining. With right sides together, sew backing with batting to front, leaving 7-inch opening along one short edge. Trim seam allowances.

5 Turn table runner right side out; press. Stitch opening closed. Smooth table runner flat and, using safety pins, pin baste the 3 layers together for quilting. To quilt, set sewing machine on long stitch length and outline-stitch the fabric pattern. Or quilt by hand, keeping fabric taut in an embroidery hoop.

FABRIC SHOWER CURTAIN

A fabric shower curtain is easy to make, and prettier than plastic.

YOU WILL NEED

- ❑ FABRIC
- ❑ SEWING MACHINE
- ❑ PINS & THREAD
- ❑ TAILOR'S CHALK
- ❑ GROMMET KIT
- ❑ WOOD BLOCK
- ❑ HAMMER & RULER
- ❑ 12 BEADED CHAINS
- ❑ SHOWER CURTAIN LINER
- ❑ IRON

BEFORE YOU BEGIN

The curtain is 12 inches wider than the rod; unfinished length is equal to distance from the rod to the floor.

Knowing Your Tools

A grommet kit, available at crafts stores, contains a circular base (A), a cylinder cutting tool (B), a tapered tool for inserting the grommets (C), grommet fronts with shafts (D) and grommet backs (E).

Piecing Fabric Together

If you're not using a bedsheet, and the chosen fabric isn't wide enough, piece it together.

On a large work surface, place the two lengths of fabric to be pieced on top of each other so that right sides are together. Line up the selvage edges so that they are matching.

Selvage

Fold the top fabric back about 1 inch to see how the pattern falls. Slide the top layer of fabric to the left or right until the patterns match. Press the top edge of the selvage down.

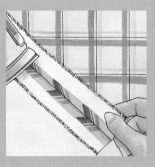

Now fold the selvage back and flatten out. Pin the selvages together along the pressed fold, making sure fabrics do not slip and the match remains true. Stitch along the fold line.

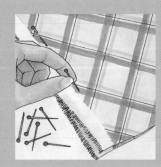

Sewing the Shower Curtain

1 Finish edges of curtain. For side hems, turn under ½ inch, then 1 inch, pin, press and top-stitch close to fold. For top and bottom hems, turn under 1 inch, then 3 inches, press, pin and topstitch close to fold.

2 Measure and mark the grom-met holes ¾ inches from top edge on wrong side of curtain. Evenly space the holes along the width of the fabric so they match up with a shower curtain liner.

3 Place wood block on a hard surface. Place top of curtain over block, centering a mark. Place the cutting edge of cylin-der on mark. Hammer cylinder to cut hole.

TAKE NOTE

For best results, practice making the grommet holes and inserting the grom-mets on scraps of fabric before making the shower curtain.

OOPS

If a grommet hole frays, spray a little adhesive over the threads to prevent fur-ther unraveling.

4 Finish cutting all holes. Pick out grommet backs and fronts. Place the shower curtain wrong side up on working sur-face. Place one grommet front on the circular metal base.

5 Carefully slide metal base and grommet front underneath the first hole in the shower curtain. Make sure the grommet front doesn't slide out of position on metal base so the grommet front and back will line up. Push grommet shaft through the hole. Then slip a grom-met back over grommet shaft.

6 Using the tapered tool, insert point through grommet shaft and hammer bulb end until the shaft flattens and folds over the back, securing grommet in place.

7 Repeat process to insert the grommets in the remaining holes. Place liner on curtain back and line up holes. Slip a beaded chain through the matched grommet and shower curtain liner holes and close. Slip shower curtain rod through chains to hang. Or snap chains around rod after it is in place.

INDEX